The Canadian Senate:
A Lobby From Within

To the memory of Mary and Jack

The Canadian Senate: A Lobby From Within

Colin Campbell

Canadian Controversies Series

Macmillan of Canada

Canadian Cataloguing in Publication Data

Campbell, Edwin Colin, 1943-
    The Canadian Senate

(Canadian controversies series)

Includes index. .
ISBN 0-7705-1695-5 bd.   ISBN 0-7705-1631-9 pa.

1. Canada. Parliament. Senate. I. Title.
II. Series.

JL155.C34   328.71'07'1   C78-001099-X

Printed in Canada for
The Macmillan Company of Canada Limited
70 Bond Street
Toronto, Ontario
M5B 1X3

Contents

Canadian Controversies Series

Canadian political commentators have adopted the full range of political styles, from cold detachment to partisan advocacy. The Canadian Controversies Series is disciplined by the idea that while political analysis must be based on sound descriptive and explanatory modes of thought, social scientists should not abnegate the role of evaluating political systems. Such evaluations require a conscious approach to the interrelationships between facts and values, empirical and normative considerations in politics.

Each theme in the series has been chosen to illustrate some basic principles of Canadian political life and to allow the respective authors freedom to develop normative positions on the related problems. It is hoped that the volumes will stimulate debate and advance public understanding of some of the major questions which confront the Canadian political system. By treating the enduring themes and problems in Canada, the authors will also illustrate the important contribution that social science can offer to politics in terms of facts, ideas, theories, and comparative frameworks within which meaningful controversy can take place. Creative political thought must not be divorced from the political fabric of a country but form an integral part of it.

ROBERT J. JACKSON
General Editor

Acknowledgments

These acknowledgments read like a litany. There are so many people who played critical roles while I wrote this book that I am compelled at least to mention their names. In particular, however, profound gratitude goes to Allan Kornberg who directed my dissertation on the Senate. Professor Kornberg, along with his colleague William Mishler, also permitted me to use data in this book from their interview study of MPs. Many of these data have appeared recently in Professors Kornberg and Mishler's *Influence in Parliament: Canada* (Durham, N.C., 1976).

Numerous people helped me at other stages of this project. Among the key people while I conducted the interviews in Ottawa were Senator Jacques Flynn, Senator Keith Davey, Ron Lefebvre, Jeanne Brown, Jean Carrière, Jean-Pierre Gaboury, Eric Spicer, and Lloyd Heaslip. Michael Kirby and Michel Rochon, both of the Prime Minister's Office, provided invaluable information on the nomination of candidates for seats in the Senate.

During the data processing and analysis I was greatly assisted by the advice of Bernard Babbitt, Susan Schiffman, Katherine Meyer, and John Seidler, and the services of the Duke University, University of North Carolina, Washington State University, University of Ottawa, University of California, and York University computer centres. Karen Dolmatch and George Shulman worked as research assistants.

Several people made editorial comments on various drafts of this book. Above all, I owe an immense debt to Marilyn Landau. A free-lance editor based in Berkeley, Ms. Landau breathed life into many of these pages. Having edited numerous social science manuscripts, she was able as well to challenge a number of my assertions and insist that I clarify several points. Barbara Werner and Anna-Marie Conklin also edited sections of the manuscript. The editor of this series, Robert Jackson, and an anonymous reader provided two excellent critiques of the first draft. Virgil Duff, Margaret Woollard, Roy Trueman, and Lloyd Elmer at Macmillan of Canada highlighted some points and made the final editorial suggestions.

Helpful professors, colleagues, and friends during the preparation of the book include William Mishler, Harold Clarke, Thomas Reese, sj, Jacques Monet, sj, Nelson W. Polsby, Robert Presthus, Fred Fletcher, Robert Drummond, Donald V. Smiley, Thomas D. Stanley, Frederick Engelmann, Joe Clark, mp, Donald Blake, Robert Gilsdorf, W. F. and Helen Dawson, Lynda Erickson, Lynda Hodges, Byron Shafer, and the late James Lee. My financial support has come mostly from Duke University, York University, the Canada Council, and the Oregon Province of the Society of Jesus. Millie Moreland, Jane Rogers, Ruth V. Halley, and Leleith Smith all tried their hands at converting my hieroglyphics into the typewritten word. They performed miracles. Several of my fellow Jesuits, especially at Chapel Hill, N.C., at The Jesuit School of Theology at Berkeley, and at Bellarmine Residence in Toronto, put up with my inattentiveness to community needs (and, indeed, gave me immense support) throughout this project.

I have dedicated this book to the memory of my parents, my first political-science teachers. When I was eight, my mother assuaged my fears that a woman could never fill the shoes of George vi by telling me that the monarch has no real power in Canada. A few months later, my father told me that I would have to become a lawyer if I wanted to be a politician. I hope that this book on the Senate makes up for my eventually becoming a priest and a political scientist!

COLIN CAMPBELL
Toronto, 1978

1.   The Senate's Role in Perspective

Here we have to remember that quality and quantity both go to the making of every state. By "quality" we mean free birth, wealth, culture, and nobility of descent, by "quantity" we mean superiority in numbers. . . . Quantity and quality must thus be placed in balance against each other. . . . Where superiority of the rich and notables in point of quality is greater than their inferiority in point of quantity, there will be an oligarchy . . .   Aristotle[1]

[Canadian Senator] Richard Deveraux had never been a statesman, either young or elder, or even a serious legislator. His chosen field was political manipulation and he had practiced it all his life. He enjoyed the exercise of semi-autonomous power. Within his party he had wielded authority as few others before him. There had been nothing sinister about this. It was based simply upon two factors— a natural political astuteness which in the past had made his advice eagerly sought, plus judicious use of money.

           Arthur Hailey[2]

The Gallup Poll of Canada asked a cross-section of Canadians, in 1951 and 1961, if they thought that the Senate did a satisfactory job. One might expect—since negative views of the Senate are not uncommon, at least among academics—that the overwhelming majority answered "No". Yet, in 1951, 50 per cent of Gallup's respondents said that they thought the Senate performed satisfactorily.[3] By 1961, this proportion had increased to 55 per cent. In 1964, however, when Gallup asked Canadians to evaluate the performance of Parliament as a

1

whole, 45 per cent said Parliament was doing a "poor job", while only 16 per cent said it was doing a "good job".[4] Thus, there was a great discrepancy between support for the Senate and for Parliament as a whole.

Possibly in 1951 and 1961 respondents benignly tolerated the Senate. Indeed, fewer than half could accurately describe at least one task it performed. Perhaps the majority had judged the Senate on the grounds of the conventional wisdom that because senators are appointed rather than elected they are powerless and, therefore, harmless.

For readers who believe that the Senate is harmless this book will be a challenge, for it takes a uniquely critical look at the institution. This chapter will study the Senate, especially since 1960, and confront the reader with the question whether it should be reformed or abolished. Analysis of the Senate's role will go beyond the usual sort of study in which the Senate is described as performing two legislative functions, namely, technical review of legislation and special studies of political problems. It will point out the degree to which the Senate operates (and does so effectively) as a lobby from within. That is, the Upper House serves mostly as a useful base of operations for legislators who employ technical review and special studies mainly on behalf of Canada's business community. This bias in the Senate's work results from two features of the Senate as an institution: senators are appointed with guaranteed tenure until age seventy-five; and they very often hold leadership positions in corporations, including director-ships. It would not be unfair to say, then, that this legislative body, shaped as it is by these two institutional features, gives an undemocratic advantage to business interests in their efforts to compete with other groups for influence in the policy arena.

This chapter also looks into the possibility of Senate reform as a means of bringing more balance to the role of the Upper House. On the basis of a study of reform attempts since Confederation, it finds that there is little likelihood that reform of the Senate, short of election of members, would bring the desired results. On the other hand, an elective second chamber would present a serious obstacle to the smooth operation of the parliamentary system. Thus, abolition appears to be the wisest course. A "House of Provinces" consisting of delegates from each province would replace the Senate and fulfil the function for which the Upper House was originally instituted but which it never really performed—the representation of provincial interests in Ottawa.

THE SENATE AS A SECOND CHAMBER: THE EXPECTATIONS OF THE FOUNDING FATHERS

Second chambers in parliamentary systems perform the whole gamut of legislative functions. Many constitutions, in addition, specify that second chambers should give priority to the two major concerns of general legislative review and protection of state, provincial, and regional rights.

The term "general legislative review" refers to the watchdog role second chambers play, rather than to their lawmaking roles in some federal systems. In theory, one main justification for upper houses has been that they protect the interests of the conservative and propertied sectors.[5] In parliamentary systems such as Canada's the general legislative function has taken the form of the "sober second thought" rather than the vetoing of bills which have won the support of the Lower House.[6] The second chambers, thus, modify legislation so that it better accommodates specific concerns of conservative or vested interests.[7] Their actual partisanship notwithstanding, members of second chambers sometimes view themselves as the appropriate legislators to study the major social and political problems of the day and to shape policies that will reflect these concerns. If they have lighter schedules than members of the Lower House, members of second chambers believe that they can do a great deal to ease the work load of a parliament.

Many constitutions mandate their second chambers to perform federal as well as general legislative roles. Six western democratic states have developed second chambers to represent and protect particular regions from the power of a majority in popularly elected national legislatures.[8] Since such representation and protection was given at the time of Confederation as the main function of Canada's Senate, it merits special consideration here. Indeed, the Senate's 104 seats divide according to regional quotas, with Ontario and Quebec receiving 24 seats each; British Columbia, Alberta, Saskatchewan, and Manitoba 6 seats each; Nova Scotia and New Brunswick 10 each; Prince Edward Island 4; Newfoundland 6; and the Northwest Territories and the Yukon 1 each.

Canada's Fathers of Confederation spent fully six days in conference about the Upper House; yet, they developed such a vulnerable institution that it is difficult to ascertain whether they really intended the Senate to play a very strong role.[9] Statements made by three key figures of the conference show that the Founding Fathers were greatly concerned with protecting provincial and sectional interests, and that they sought a mechanism in the proposed federal union which would do just this.

John A. Macdonald, the Conservative leader and a future Prime Minister, said about the need for an Upper House:

> In order to protect local interests, and to prevent sectional jealousies, it was found requisite that the great divisions into which British North America is separated should be represented in the Upper House on the principle of equality.[10]

George-Etienne Cartier, the chief French-speaking participant, added that an Upper House would assure the protection of the French-Canadian minority.[11] Finally, the Upper-Canadian Grit, George Brown, said that establishment of the Senate was essential to the bargain being struck between Lower Canada (Quebec) and the English-speaking colonies.[12] Representation by population, he suggested, gave the English a clear majority in the Lower House, while weighted representation in the Upper House would protect French interests. For all their concern, however, the Founding Fathers believed that the Senate should perform protection of sectional interests only within limits. Macdonald said that the Senate *"will never see itself in opposition against the deliberate and understood wishes of the people"*.[13] George Brown even said that the Upper House would have to refrain from vetoing money bills.[14]

Some authors have thus concluded that Ontario's representatives to the founding conference created the Senate as a ploy to lure other partners to Confederation.[15] These authors point to the Senate's secondary roles as proof of this hypothesis. The Upper House was to serve secondarily as: (1) "a check upon the Lower House, and hence upon the encroachment of democracy", and (2) a protector of the interests of property.[16] More likely, however, the Fathers' ambivalence about the machinery required for effective regional representation, rather than political sabotage, would explain the tenuity of the Senate's ultimate institutional position. At the time of Confederation it seemed appropriate to argue for limits to the Senate's power to veto legislation on behalf of the provinces. In the United States, for example, sectional interests seemed to have exploited their "weighted" representation in the Senate to the detriment of "good" government. Upper Canadians, as well, dismissed their elected Upper House as redundant. Finally, the belief was widely held among the Fathers "that sectional representation in the Cabinet, backed by its representatives in the Commons, would control the appointments to the Upper Chamber",[17] and consequently provide adequately for the safeguarding of provincial and sectional interests.[18] The Fathers tried to design an institution which, first, would not undermine Confederation and, second, would foster provincial representation. As we will see, they created a Senate which fulfils only the first of their objectives.

THE SENATE SINCE CONFEDERATION: ITS ACTUAL ROLE

An Historical Overview

Although the Senate has the constitutional powers of amendment and veto over all bills from the House of Commons, the British North America Act denies it several powers as well. The Upper House has no powers that are exclusive from those of the House of Commons; nor can it originate bills for the raising or spending of money.[19] Since senators are summoned by the Governor General at the request of the Prime Minister, the Upper House lacks the electoral power base held by second chambers in some federal systems. The Senate's effectiveness and public image have been additionally damaged by the practice of appointment for life (until mandatory retirement at seventy-five came into effect in 1966). The Senate has been subject, then, to what one author has termed a "context of subordination".[20] Although its legislative powers remain on paper as strong as they were in 1867, in practice the Upper House has become hesitant in its use of its more potent weapons, the amendment and veto of legislation. For instance, whereas the Senate amended 25 per cent and rejected 8 per cent of bills from the House of Commons during the period 1867-73, it amended only 3.5 per cent and rejected only 1.2 per cent during 1963-74.[21]

In view of its reluctance to confront the House of Commons directly, what has the Senate done since 1867? MacKay for one says it has done little to champion provincial or sectional rights:[22] (1) in an early battle over the extension of the franchise, the Senate "switched sides from time to time" between the provinces and the federal government; (2) it delayed or rejected legislation requested by particular provinces; (3) it complied with the federal government's policy with regard to separate schools in the provinces; (4) only irregularly did it support provincial wishes to limit the scope of railroad regulation; (5) it overlooked parochial interests in 1912 and 1913 when it supported the view that federal funds for highways should be equitably apportioned; and, (6) it gave short shrift to Quebec's sectional concerns during the conscription crisis of the First World War.

Kunz describes the Senate's federal role more generously.[23] He suggests that the Upper House has failed to champion provincial interests for four clear reasons. First of all, he says, early judicial decisions assured a certain amount of provincial rights. Second, provincial representation on the federal Cabinet protects sectional interests. Third, provincial governments often make themselves adequately heard at federal-provincial conferences. Fourth, voters in provinces often elect provincial governments of a different party from the government party in Ottawa. Provincial voters often believe that such governments will take stronger provincial-rights stances in their dealings with the federal government.

Kunz goes on to show that the Senate has helped the provinces when called upon. But some of the examples he gives to make this point seem contradictory. He cites, for example, the fact that the Senate vetoed a 1936 amendment to the BNA Act which would have enabled the provinces to levy indirect taxes. The dubious ground for this Senate veto was that the amendment would have curtailed the constitutional powers of the federal government. Kunz cites other legislation in which the Senate acted in behalf of provincial interests. In 1925, the Senate amended a relatively minor bill, Canteen Funds Distribution, in favour of the provinces; it stipulated that $2,300,000 owed to returning First World War veterans should be distributed through the existing machinery of the provinces. The Senate, as well, made two revisions to the 1935 Criminal Code at the request of provincial governments. First, it deleted Paragraph F, which made it an offense to deduct funds from any employee's wages unless a competent public authority approved such a deduction. Second, it made stronger the laws controlling the operation of gambling devices at public resorts. The Senate also saw to it in 1940 that, before the RCMP could police municipalities, the provincial governments had to approve all relevant contracts. Finally, in an amendment to the Northwest Territories Bill, the Senate stipulated that eight provincial courts, rather than the Ontario Superior Court alone, would exercise jurisdiction in civil matters over the Northwest Territories.

With respect to its general legislative role, the Senate, as we have seen, eschews the nineteenth-century view that it must frequently amend and veto legislation if it is to serve as the bulwark of propertied and conservative interests against the "liberal" legislation of the House of Commons. Some students of the Senate, indeed, maintain that its general legislative role no longer contains a conservative bias. Kunz, for instance, summarizes the present role as consisting of two tasks.[24] First, the Senate limits the extension of ministerial discretion if this can be done without jeopardizing the underlying policy upon which a bill is based. Second, the Upper House assures that the enactment of legislation does not trample on the interests and the rights of the ordinary person.

Two cases exemplify for Kunz the respective senatorial general-legislative roles.[25] These are the Customs Tariffs Bill (1961) and the Bank of Canada Bill (1961). The Customs Tariffs Bill gave the Minister of National Revenue absolute discretion over the rates of customs duties. Taking the position that the legislation would lodge too much power in the bureaucracy, the Senate therefore amended the bill to make ministerial rate fixing appealable to the Tariff Board. The Bank of Canada Bill attempted to oust the Governor of the Bank of Canada, James E. Coyne, by Act of Parliament and without a hearing. The Senate gave Mr. Coyne "his day in court" before the Banking, Trade, and Commerce Committee. These cases, however, hardly justify Kunz's conclusion that the Senate "has acted in the capacity of a sort of institutional Ombudsman in the Canadian parliamentary system".[26] These actions occurred during a period when the Progressive Conservative Prime Minister, John Diefenbaker, had his large majority of seats in the House of Commons, while the Liberals held a majority of seats in the Senate. The Senate's boldness stemmed from extremely partisan motives,[27] and from mounting concern that Diefenbaker's financial policies were deleterious to the Canadian business community.

Indeed it is precisely such incidents of lobbying for the cause of business which point to a highly significant general legislative role which often has been overlooked by political pundits and scholars, Kunz included. A later section will illustrate that, by employing their legal and financial expertise, senators have played an important part in drafting corrections and/or administrative improvements which make legislation much more favourable to the business community. The process usually does not necessitate the Senate's passing amendments of bills against the wishes of the government. It involves rather incorporating into bills provisions that are requested by members of the business community for whom senators have gained a sympathetic hearing from the government. We may term this legislative role "business review", that is, systematic review of legislation from the standpoint of the interests of business. The Senate's success in this role applies both to legislation that it studies before an actual bill has been passed by the House of Commons, and to legislation of a complex or highly technical nature that is introduced in the Upper House and reviewed in depth before being passed and sent to the Lower House. In the former situation, the government itself usually sponsors Senate-proposed amendments while the bill is still in the House of Commons. In the latter situation, it likewise sponsors amendments, but while the bill is still in the Senate.

THE SENATE'S ROLE IN PERSPECTIVE: SOME RECENT TRENDS

Canadian senators and their roles are often poorly understood. Political scientists and political journalists must shoulder some of the responsibility for confused public perceptions of senators. With the exception of some Senate watchers, authors often fail to inform readers of the Senate's role in the legislative process or to point out the options open to individual senators to influence that process. When political writers do take the Senate into account they tell their readers that senators perform three tasks, two of which are *legislative*, one of which is *political*. With respect to their political function, senators accept appointments to the Upper House; in this way they make room for new blood in the Cabinet or the House of Commons, both of which are considered more vital areas of political life than the Senate.[28] This political function then is characterized by many as simply restorative. With respect to the two legislative functions, senators scrutinize and refine the "details" and "language" of legislation;[29] they also study the problems of society and of the political system.[30] Yet even authors who concern themselves with the Senate fail to elaborate adequately upon senatorial roles so as to leave the reader with an accurate idea of what senators do.

This section will attempt to clarify senators' two legislative roles, particularly since 1960. First, however, it will briefly challenge conventional wisdom about senators' political functions.

Peter C. Newman challenges the view that senators' political roles are simply restorative. He describes a variety of substantive political activities which senators engage in.[31] Newman portrays senators as the top advisors, the "backstage boys", and the "managerial elite" of Prime Ministers; the builders of national party organizations; the chief fund raisers; the prime-ministerial "kingmakers"; and the chief plotters in palace revolts. The facts support Newman: the last five presidents of the Liberal Federation of Canada have been members of the Senate;[32] several senators head their party organizations in their provinces; and many members, most notably Keith "The Rainmaker" Davey, have engineered impressive election victories for their party.

F. C. Engelmann and Mildred Schwartz agree with Newman in their assertion that senators who are sympathetic to a Prime Minister can help him maintain control of the parliamentary party's caucus.[33] Engelmann and Schwartz also claim that individual senators can have a great impact on the over-all operation of their parties' organizations:

> Often senators from the provinces are agents of the governing party in Ottawa; they handle its finances in their home province, or conduct its campaigns. In such cases, their function is to attempt to bring the provincial electorate in line with the nationally favored party.[34]

K. Z. Paltiel, in addition, argues that, at least since Mackenzie King, senators have played key fund-raising roles in the national organizations of parties.[35]

BUSINESS REVIEW

By looking into the Senate at work on business review, one looks right into the heart of Canadian liberal democracy. Here the business community applies subtle and not-so-subtle pressure for adaptations of government legislation to fit their viewpoint. Senators play crucial roles in the process. In a very real sense they are the lobby from within. They bargain and negotiate on business's behalf for amendments which are essential for a favourable financial and commercial climate. When the government refuses to accommodate certain business claims, senators can convey to business the "necessity" of the government policy.

This section discusses several bills which the Senate has considered since 1960 which indicate just how business review works. Along the way we will see how senators manoeuvre, bargain, and use subtle tactics to accommodate legislation to the business viewpoint. The mechanisms involved are part and parcel of the art of lobbying. This section does not pretend to assert for the first time that business groups lobby in Ottawa, or even that senators give them greater access to the policy arena than other groups have. To appreciate these pages fully, however, the reader must keep in mind the fact that senators' lobbying activities are paid for by the people of Canada and not by the business firms and groups whose interests they advance. Further, senators do not have to face periodic elections which, presumably, would strain out members who represent business to the virtual exclusion of all other interests. The pages which follow, thus, reveal the type of one-sided review which takes place in a legislature created by a political system which bends over backwards to ensure that business has preferential access to the policy process. The system provides extreme accommodation, of course, by paying the salaries of business lobbyists, giving them full membership in the community of legislators, and protecting them from public review of their tenure.

The fact that business review mainly involves technical details of legislation does not diminish its importance. Since 1867, most legislation has handled administrative matters rather than innovative policy.[36] This phenomenon is largely due to the rationalistic "style" of Canadian politics, a style which does not lend itself easily to radical legislative initiatives. Like the United States, Canada is a political environment where the marketplace ethic prevails and where most decisions are made through "partisan mutual adjustment".[37]

The Senate's Banking, Trade, and Commerce Committee conducts most business review. Headed by Senator Salter Hayden (a top corporation lawyer and businessman), the committee gained attention in 1961 when it aimed a vigorous attack on the Customs Tariffs and Bank of Canada bills. In 1964, the Banking Committee demanded and won approval of three amendments to the Companies Bill. These amendments stated that: (1) individuals and companies trading corporate shares need not report these transactions publicly; (2) the Secretary of State may not instigate prosecution against disputing shareholders unless one or other of the parties concerned initiates legal action; and (3) the provisions of the bill must be in keeping with current provincial statutes. Such alterations demonstrate how the Banking Committee, although it usually cloaks its ideological conservatism in concern with technical matters, presses for changes which, when adopted, can significantly reduce the force of regulatory legislation.

The Banking Committee has come under fire from the media for another bias in its legislative review, a disinclination to approve bills which would decentralize Canadian banking. In 1964, for example, it pigeonholed three bills which granted charters for three banks: a Bank of Western Canada, a Laurentide Bank, and a Bank of British Columbia. Not only were there already enough banks in Canada, several senators argued, but the Bank of British Columbia threatened free enterprise as well, because the government of British Columbia would control it. When the press discovered, however, that four members of the Banking Committee held directorships in charter banks, they charged conflict of interest.[38] The four senators succumbed to public pressure and disqualified themselves from the vote.[39] (Motivated by recollection of this episode, four senators disqualified themselves in 1976-77 from the Banking Committee's review of a major bank act.) The charters for the Bank of Western Canada and the Laurentide Bank thus passed through committee. The latter-proposed bank, however, was assigned a higher required capital than it had anticipated. The Bank of British Columbia eventually won approval by Parliament in 1966.

In 1968, the Banking Committee again tried to check the growth of ministerial regulation of business. This time its proposed amendments to the Hazardous Products Bill passed the Senate but were so extensive that the bill as a whole died in the House of Commons. But when the Commons revived the bill in 1969, incorporating into it many of the Senate's original amendments, the Senate balked once again. This time it refused to pass the bill until three more amendments were added. Proposed by the Banking Committee, these called for: (1) greater flexibility in the specifications for product inspectors; (2) a two-year lifetime for new product names appearing on the hazardous substances list; and (3) a sixty-day appeal period during which manufacturers would state their cases before the Hazardous Products Board of Review. The first and third amendments passed the Senate, while part of the second was incorporated in the bill by the Commons. Thus, the Banking Committee's review, in the long run, was able to limit substantially ministerial discretion in the regulation of hazardous products.

The Senate Banking Committee had even further success in protecting the interests of the business community with the Investment Companies Bill of 1969. An investment company is one that borrows money from the public in the form of notes, debentures, and bonds, and then either invests these funds in other businesses or loans the money without security. The bill gave the federal government licence to monitor the activities of investment companies in the name of consumer protection. The Banking Committee, however, saw the bill as a threat to the financial sector; they charged that it encouraged government encroachment in private affairs. The process of change that the bill then went through illuminates the subtle way in which senators work to modify legislation in favour of particular interests; their methods (as we shall see) are delay, debate, and endless "technical" amendment on the one hand, and hasty approval in the eleventh hour of the process on the other.

The Banking Committee first drastically rewrote the first draft of the bill (s-17, 1969), employing at private expense a team of part-time legal advisors to draft the amendments.[40] A delay then resulted, so that the legislation did not pass Parliament that year. When the bill was reintroduced as c-3 through the Commons the following October, the Banking Committee proposed even further amendments. These amendments ruled that: (1) manufacturing companies did not have to comply with the "surveillance" legislation if they owned subsidiaries which in turn themselves owned subsidiaries; (2) car manufacturing companies with sales finance and acceptance companies "downstream" would likewise not have to comply with the surveillance; (3) mandatory review of all sales of companies' shares abroad would be limited to situations where the entire operation of the corporation in Canada is alienated to foreign interests; (4) auditors who report to the government on their company's condition would be immune from prosecution; (5) money advanced by chartered banks to the Canada Deposit Insurance Corporation (a public insurance corporation for bank security) would not be used as security for investment companies; and (6) ministerial discretion in the administration of the bill would be weakened.

These changes illustrate the manner in which the Senate can dilute legislation in order to protect particular interests in the private sector.[41] Senator Hayden gives us further insight into this process by revealing how the first two amendments came to be.[42] The first amendment was added, he tells us, because three of Canada's largest manufacturing and holding companies, Labatt's, Molson's, and Weston's pressed their objections to the bill in the Senate after their representations to the government and the House of Commons had failed. The second amendment was adopted by the Senate because the automobile companies convinced the Banking Committee of what they had not been able to persuade the government: that car dealers who have difficulty raising capital benefit when manufacturers lend them money. Such loans, the Banking Committee concluded, are "temporary and incidental to the principal business of the shareholder".

We see here how pressure subtly and cleverly applied in the right places helps advance the interests of the business community. First, individuals make their interests known to the civil servants who draft the legislation. Then they take their case to the House of Commons committee. If they do not get a favourable response there, they then try to convince the Senate's Banking Committee that their views are reasonable and deserve support. If they succeed here, Senator Hayden and some of his colleagues confer with and court the approval of the civil servant in charge of the legislation. If they win him over, most likely the Cabinet Minister to whom the civil servant reports will likewise give his assent to the amendment, and it will probably pass the Senate without offending the government. It was in this way that Bill c-3 won Senate approval and finally passed in the House of Commons.

Another example of this process is the Senate's eleventh-hour passing of the Income Tax Act (c-259) in December of 1971. While the legislation grants relief to some taxpayers, it increases taxes in higher-income brackets and introduces capital-gains taxation for the first time. Robert Presthus asserts that the bill serves as a clear instance of government policy's being "sharply modified by systematic interest group action".[43]

The story of the bill's review in Parliament begins with the White Paper on taxation. The House of Commons Finance Committee received 520 briefs during its review of the White Paper. Even in this forum those who opposed the bill commanded much more attention than the economically disadvantaged who stood to gain the most from tax reform.[44] Opponents of tax reform found another receptive audience in the Senate. The Banking Committee, thus, received 343 submissions and incorporated them into a ninety-page report.

When the actual Income Tax Reform Bill reached the Commons in 1971, the Senate Banking Committee immediately began a preparatory study of the legislation. This study was undertaken when several senators complained that they rarely had sufficient time to review Commons bills which affected business. They cited the 1963 Income Tax Bill and the 1967 Bank Bill as examples. In 1963, many senators had wanted to provide a tax shelter for foreign investments in disadvantaged areas of Canada; in 1967, however, some senators had wanted to delete or mitigate a section which limited the number of interlocking directorships that bank officers could hold. In the case of the 1971 Tax Bill, Senator Hayden had concluded that the Upper House is entitled to study a bill as soon as it reaches the Commons, since the Senate tables all information concerning newly introduced bills.[45] When the preparatory study got under way, the Banking Committee heard from 129 witnesses and filed three interim reports over a period of several months.

The Banking Committee was exceptionally successful in one sense. The government bill incorporated forty-four of the Senate's original proposals for improvements of the White Paper.[46] Once the government bill was introduced in the committee, however, the committee's channels seemed to be partially closed off. The government was in a hurry to have the bill approved in December 1971 so that it would apply during the following tax year. The Minister of Finance, Edgar Benson, simply would not endorse some of the recommendations which the committee had viewed as essential to the bill. Although some senators were prepared to resist this move on the part of the government, prudence ultimately won out. The Banking Committee and the Senate passed the bill within the constraints set by the "Christmas" recess.

The press charged the Senate with "rubber-stamping". Some imaginative journalists even predicted that the Upper House was threatened with abolition if it failed to meet the government deadline.[47] The media, apparently, were not paying close attention to events in the Banking Committee.[48] Edgar Benson had simply convinced the senators that the government had not considered fully the consequences of the committee's unaccepted recommendations. The government, in particular, did not know what effect the proposed amendments would have on revenues. Indeed, by April 1973, a new Minister of Finance, John Turner, appeared before the Banking Committee with a package of amendments which responded to all of the key recommendations of the committee. Parliament enacted all of these retroactively to January 1, 1972. Briefly, the principal amendments: (1) allowed for greater discretion in donors' valuation of gifts; (2) provided that capital-gains taxes not be levied on beneficiaries of profit-sharing plans until the holdings are disposed of; (3) curtailed for at least another two years the foreign-accrual property income tax; (4) exempted from the law certain classes of non-resident investors; (5) permitted the payment of capital-gains taxes in instalments for up to six years; and (6) dispensed from the Act's departure-tax rules those who had been resident in Canada for less than thirty-six months.

After this success, the Banking Committee has since conducted preparatory studies of several bills. In 1973, for example, the committee studied a bill restricting foreign investment in Canada. Hayden led the committee through a slow-paced study during which he established a new ground rule for its relations with the government. In one of his more testy statements, he said that his committee refused to succumb to "Christmas closures" like the one which occurred in 1971.[49] The committee made fourteen recommendations.[50] Six of these were incorporated and four others were partially accommodated. With respect to the latter, the then Minister of Industry, Trade, and Commerce, Alistair Gillespie, promised an ongoing review of the operation of the act to see if the senators' remaining objections should be met by further amendments.

By studying bills before they reach the Upper House, the committee has kept a sharp eye on bills which affect business. This has been its greatest influence. Perhaps even more than the members of the Commons Finance Committee, the Senate Banking Committeemen, through astute use of expertise and privileges, have learned the art of political bargaining and are accomplished at negotiating with government representatives to gain their ends.

Competing with the Banking Committee in recent years for some of its work has been the Senate National Finance Committee. Douglas Everett, its chairman since 1970, has directed much of the committee's energy to business review. Before that it was considered only a sinecure for aging senators or a stepping stone to the Banking Committee. In and of itself it had little influence even after 1964 when it began to review appropriations on a regular basis. Then in 1971, under Everett, the Finance Committee studied the impact government financial policies had on growth, employment, and price stability in the

Canadian economy.[51] As a result of the study, the committee expressed concern that government too frequently impinges upon the free marketplace. It recommended, thus, that the federal government make four modifications to its program of intervention to alleviate the effects of inflation. These four recommendations were: (1) wage and price controls should not be used unless a strong national consensus develops in their favour; (2) Canada's foreign exchange rate should continue to float so as to control the importation of inflation; (3) the government should adopt high-employment budgets, assuring only 4–4.5 per cent unemployment, and should take special measures on behalf of those who remain disadvantaged; and (4) the government should attempt to hold increases in the Consumer Price Index to between 2 and 3 per cent annually and should peg increments in social benefits to this rate. The report anticipated, in broad outline, the financial policy which the Liberals followed from 1971 to the introduction of wage and price controls in October 1975. Indeed, as a barometer of thinking in the business community, the committee probably retarded the government's adoption of mandatory controls to combat inflation.

After the inflation study the Finance Committee shifted its attention to individual governmental programs which seemed to be in fiscal trouble. In 1973 it embarked on an intensive study of Information Canada with an eye to improving its efficiency. Information Canada was the agency that handled all publication of documents for the federal government. As a result of the study, the committee proposed changes to improve the agency's operation as well as to streamline media use in all the ministries and agencies of government.[52] (The government ultimately dismantled Information Canada in 1976.) In 1975, the committee investigated, from a financial viewpoint, the training and placement services provided by the Department of Manpower and Immigration. During 1976-77 it has been studying federal government rentals of office space from private corporations.

The rentals investigation follows on the heels of charges that the Liberal government has shown favouritism to the Campeau Corporation in the financial arrangements for a multimillion dollar federal office complex across the Ottawa River from

Parliament in Hull, Quebec. It is fair to ask whether the Finance Committee will conduct its inquiry impartially. During the fiscal year 1974-75, eight senators were directors on the boards of twelve companies which rented space to the federal government. Three of these senators were listed as members of the Finance Committee when the inquiry began, including Senator Louis de G. Giguère. Senator Giguère, until the allegations of his involvement in the "Sky Shops Affair" in the Fall of 1975, served as a director of Campeau. The corporation, during the fiscal year 1974-75, received 10.1 of the 15.3 million dollars that the federal government gave for rentals from companies with senators as directors.[53]

SOCIAL INVESTIGATION

Students of the Senate often dismiss social investigation as "busywork" for part-time legislators with little to do. Yet, during the late 1960s and early 1970s, social investigation became integral to the ultimate development of innovative policy. Senators used committee studies in that period to influence acceptance of new social policies. They did this by cultivating national consensus around key issue areas. Insofar as they were successful, they offset to a degree the one-sided influence of business reviewers.

In the past, the Senate has confined most of its social investigations to special committees. In the early 1960s for example, the Special Committee on Land Use (1957-61) did much of the preparatory work for the Agriculture and Rural Development Act (ARDA) of 1961. The Diefenbaker government gave strong backing to the committee, headed by Senator A. M. Pearson, which thus had little difficulty in mobilizing support for the ARDA and which was able to see its several recommendations enacted in 1961 as legislation.[54] Also during this period, Senator David Croll's Special Committee on Manpower and Employment (1960-61) helped develop a new idea—that of an umbrella agency which would integrate all governmental activities in the training, counselling, and placement of workers. This idea became reality in 1966, when the Department of Manpower and Immigration was established.

Senator Croll was a man of considerable influence during the years when the special committee study was the mode of social investigation. He spearheaded two simultaneous studies, both of which were aimed at correcting social ills. They were the Senate Special Committee on Aging (1963-66) and the Joint Senate–House of Commons Committee on Consumer Credit (1963-67). Croll and his committeemen had special success with their Committee on Aging; of the ninety-two recommendations they presented to the government twenty-five were completely adopted and another fifty-two accepted in good part.[55] Seven of the recommendations, moreover, were put into practice right away. These were directed at solving problems in what the report called high-priority areas, and resulted in: a lowering of the minimum age for benefits to the aged; the Adult Occupational Training Act (1967); three changes in the Central Mortgage and Housing Corporation; National Housing Act loans to group rental housing for the elderly; and a reduction in the capital funds required for volunteer agencies for the aged to be eligible for government loans.

Croll was not as successful with his Joint Committee on Consumer Credit, although the committee's work did help to establish the Bureau of Consumer Affairs (1970). Ron Basford, Croll's co-chairman and an expert in the field, became the first Minister of the Department of Consumer and Corporate Affairs (1970).

Croll next turned his attention to alleviating poverty. The resulting Special Committee on Poverty (1968-71) produced several recommendations, some of which were extremely controversial.[56] The committee proposed a Guaranteed Annual Income program which eventually would be comprehensive; it suggested that the definition of the poverty line be a function of the average standard of living; it called for a Council of Applied Social Research; and it advocated uniformity among workmen's compensation programs in the various provinces.

The press focused a great deal of attention on the Poverty Committee throughout the course of its inquiry. The report itself still ranks as the all-time best seller in the category of government documents. The government, moreover, accepted the committee's Guaranteed Annual Income recommendation, but has delayed implementation, it says, until the economy improves. Senator Croll takes considerable pride in this achievement. He likes to point out, as well, that thanks to the work of his committee, the press and government have showed renewed interest in such social services as legal aid, day care, and facilities for the aging; and that several government agencies, federal as well as provincial, now employ the committee's guidelines to determine the poverty line.[57]

Senator Croll's accomplishments are in no way diminished by the fact that two other senators have had considerable success in influencing policy and focusing attention on specific issues. These are Maurice Lamontagne, an economist committed to the improvement of science policy in Canada, and Keith Davey, an advertising man and Liberal party organizer dedicated to making the media more responsive to Canadians. Their special committees, respectively, were Science Policy (1968-present) and Mass Media (1969-71).

Academics have quoted continually from Lamontagne's three Science Committee reports in recent years.[58] The reports called for three reforms in Canada's science policy: (1) the establishment of a Ministry of State for Science and Technology (MOSST) and the development of a comprehensive national science policy; (2) closer alignment of basic and applied research in Canada with industrial and social development; and (3) granting to the MOSST the authority to approve science budgets in all departments of government and to ensure that all federally funded research activities fit the goals of national development. For the most part, these policy proposals have been put into effect.

How can we explain the great success of this committee? A sceptic might suggest that Senator Lamontagne simply fitted his own interests to those of the government. Yet, as one senator has pointed out, Lamontagne followed some essential rules for the successful social investigator.[59] Lamontagne first carved out a policy area according to his talents. Next he had to win support for his study from his colleagues. Unlike business reviewers, however, he could not point to pressures from business notables who have long-standing links with the Senate to convince his colleagues that a study must be done. Instead, he had to go to the public forum and put his case before several groups, hoping that he would be able to beat support out of the woods. Once he convinced his colleagues that his issue was widely perceived as important, he gained the necessary resources and Senate time to get under way. Even with the completion of the study his work was not done. He then had to maintain interest among like-minded publics and make discreet use of his reputation in the Liberal caucus and among Cabinet Ministers to ensure that his proposals came to fruition. Social investigatory work differs then from business review in that, although it calls upon lobbying skills, it requires, in addition, that the lobbyist build and maintain the support of a national constituency which, unlike the business community, transcends sectorial divisions. Social investigation, then, is *not* lobbying *from within*.

Senator Keith Davey employed the same tactics to achieve success for his Special Committee on Mass Media.[60] Unlike Lamontagne's committee, not all of its recommendations came immediately to fruition. The government, for example, has never established a Federal Press Ownership Review Board to prevent monopolies among newspapers or periodicals. On the whole, however, many of the Media Committee's recommendations have had real repercussions on the life and health of the media in Canada.

When Senator Charles McElman of New Brunswick, for example, saw that the flap over alleged monopolies had aroused the public, he responded by stirring up support for litigation against his long-time political foe, K. C. Irving. He charged that the Irving family, New Brunswick's dominant industrialists, monopolized the English-language daily newspapers in the province. The federal government prosecuted the Irving family under the Combines Act. In January 1974, the Irvings were convicted and ordered to disband their newspaper monopoly and to pay fines totalling $150,000.

One of the things the committee had in mind when it made its proposals was to encourage within Canadian society an atmosphere that would promote a free press. This meant a press that would not only turn a keen and critical eye upon society and government but would likewise be open enough to respond to public grievances. In direct response to this committee objective, publishers in three provinces established press councils comprised of media representatives as well as of the lay public. These councils serve as forums for the media and the public to air their grievances and needs.

When Keith Davey became chairman of the Media Committee he set himself one task above all others. This was to do away with the *"Time–Reader's Digest* exemption" which provided that Canadian firms which advertised in *Time* and *Reader's Digest* did not have to pay the 20 per cent tax assessed on advertisements in other foreign-owned magazines. The St. Laurent government had established the tax in 1957 and Diefenbaker had exempted *Time* and *Reader's Digest* advertisers from it in 1958 because of heavy U.S. pressure.[61] *Time* and *Reader's Digest* advertisers, moreover, could deduct their expenses for tax purposes while advertisers in all other foreign magazines, by the Pearson government's 1965 law, could not.[62]

The issue became such an explosive one that, in 1965, Pearson's nationalistic Minister of Finance, Walter Gordon, quit his post over it. Keith Davey, every bit the nationalist Gordon is, included abolition of the *Time–Reader's Digest* exemption as a key plank in the Media Committee report. At first, the government disregarded the plank. Fate, however, was on Davey's side. As Federal Campaign Co-Chairman, he engineered a surprising landslide election victory for the Liberals in the summer of 1974, helping to maintain the Trudeau government and at the same time winning himself new leverage. He used his increased influence in his campaign against the *Time–Reader's Digest* exemption, until Parliament finally revoked it in 1976.

We have seen, then, how the Senate's special committees on social problems have wielded power, particularly during the late sixties and early seventies. But, traditionally, they have been loath to utilize this potential, especially when policy alternatives were seen as "radical". While the Poverty Committee was writing its report, for example, it suffered acute embarrassment: two of its key staff members resigned; they were angry, they said, because senators on the committee balked at a censure of Canada's political structure for perpetuating poverty. (The staff subsequently published its own report, a document entitled *The Real Poverty Report*.)[63] The staff resignations, although unfortunate for Senate prestige, illustrate the constraints under which, in common with many deliberative bodies under a parliamentary system of government, the Upper House labours. In theory, the Senate can provide a systematic and intensive airing of all controversial issues that beset Canadian society. In reality senators' investigations are constrained not only by their own innate conservatism (senators, after all, continue to be drawn from the top socio-economic strata of Canadian society) but also by a consideration of what they feel a current government is likely to find acceptable. They are undoubtedly aware that Canadian governments are slow to find proposals for drastic policy changes acceptable.

Increasingly, Senate standing committees whose subject matters are not directly related to business and finance are taking the initiative and studying certain legislative matters in depth. This is a significant departure from previous practices whereby many complex bills went to the Banking Committee regardless of their nature. The bills which went to the Banking Committee include the Criminal Code Amendment Bill (1965), the Bill to Amend the Hazardous Substances Act (which permitted the advertising of contraceptives, 1967), the Divorce Bill (1967-68), and the Bill to Amend the Food and Drugs Act (1968). The standing committees which focus on social or systemic matters have also conducted special investigations independently of specific legislative proposals (for example, Foreign Affairs' studies of relations with the Caribbean Area [1970-71], the Pacific [1970-73], Europe [1972-74], and the U.S. [1974-present]; and the Legal and Constitutional Affairs' study of Canada's parole system [1971-74]). Since 1972 a standing committee under Senator Hazen Argue has reviewed Senate agricultural legislation; since 1974 a joint Senate–House standing committee under Senator Eugene Forsey has surveyed the government's use of statutory instruments.

Recently the Legal and Constitutional Affairs Committee, under the chairmanship of Senator H. Carl Goldenberg, has in large part appropriated much of the social investigatory work which was done by special committees in the late sixties and early seventies. Government Leaders, obviously, prefer Goldenberg's low-key approach to the aggressiveness of other social investigators. This development has muted considerably the impact of individual crusades such as Croll's, Lamontagne's, and Davey's. The committee started its social investigatory work in 1969 by promoting the Hate Propaganda Bill; despite objections from conservative members on both sides of the Upper House, the bill passed the Senate in May 1970. The Legal Committee then studied the parole system, recommending that the government grant hearings to convicts who are denied paroles; the government implemented the plan.

The Legal Committee has not always sided with individual rights. In 1973, for example, it deleted a clause inserted by the House of Commons in the government's Criminal Code Bill; this clause stipulated that law enforcement agencies notify suspects within ninety days after installation of phone taps. The Legal Committee sided with the Minister of Justice, Otto Lang, stating that the inclusion of the clause in the bill would weaken the government's power to fight crime. The Commons, however, persisted in its amendment and, on January 12, 1974, the Senate passed the controversial bill intact.

The Legal Committee's enormous backlog of work testifies to the fact that it now monopolizes social investigation in the Senate. For instance, in mid-1975 the committee was conducting an in-depth study of a Senate bill to decriminalize the use and simple possession of cannabis. Several other bills were in the docket; among these were Senator Donald Cameron's gun-control bill and the Privy Council Office "Green Paper", entitled *Members of Parliament and Conflict of Interest* (1973). Meanwhile, Senator Croll was denied the conflict-of-interest study and one on the work ethic; Chesley Carter, Chairman of the Health, Welfare, and Science Committee, lost the cannabis study; and Senator Argue was denied a study on an agriculture bill. It seems that the social-investigatory impulse which emerged in the late 1960s may have been tamed. The current

Government Leader in the Senate keeps Liberal mavericks reined in, with incapacitating results for social investigation.

With respect, then, to the Senate's current legislative role, we have seen that it can wield considerable influence in two ways. First, its business-oriented review of certain measures often alters, under the guise of technical amendments, the substantive impact of legislation which attempts to regulate business or redistribute wealth. Second, its social investigation, although now apparently in decline, resulted during the late 1960s and early 1970s in several changes in social legislation. It is, I think, appropriate to ask whether, in performing the first of these functions (and particularly in view of the premature decline of the second), the current Senate does not provide too much institutionalized protection for business interests.

The section which follows points out that reform proposals which would bring greater balance to the Senate's work take so long to come to fruition, and are usually so diluted by the time they are adopted, that the Senate status quo may be considered to be unusually resistant to change.

THE ELUSIVENESS OF SENATE REFORM

Several times between Confederation and the 1960s, politicians and scholars have found themselves debating proposals for Senate reform. None of these schemes, however, has come to fruition. The Conservative party has consistently supported the Senate as a vehicle for the "sober second thought". The Liberals have, from time to time, made more or less genuine appeals for reform. From 1893 to 1927, for example, they made vague pleas for Senate reform in their party platforms.[64] During the 1920s, Liberal Prime Minister Mackenzie King sought to pass new social measures by repealing anti-union legislation and instituting an Old Age Pension program which the Conservative majority in the Senate effectively defeated. Clashes with the Senate thus intensified the Liberals' desire for reform. When the Liberals finally gained a majority in both Houses in 1943, social legislation at last began to win relatively easy approval from the Senate, and the need to press for Senate reform diminished.

The issue was not revived (by a Prime Minister) until 1961, when John Diefenbaker introduced a reform bill in reaction to the Customs Tariff Bill defeat (1960), and the Coyne Affair (1961).[65] The bill required all senators to retire at age seventy. The House of Commons never passed it. When Lester Pearson, a Liberal, took over as Prime Minister, he too proposed a retirement bill requiring all senators appointed after June 2, 1965 to retire at age seventy-five. When it passed, Pearson became the only Prime Minister to get a Senate reform bill through Parliament.

Some senators have been as critical as any outsiders of their own role. Alexander, in 1882, and McMullen, David, and Beique, in 1908, all argued for reform. By 1917, senators mandated a special committee study on reform of the Upper House. The results of the study, however, were less than spectacular. The committee report simply reasserted the Senate's power to amend money bills downwards. In response, the Upper House established the Standing Committee on Finance which ultimately improved Senate review of government estimates.

After the 1917 study, the issue of reform remained dormant within the Senate until 1934. The Government Leader, Arthur Meighen, advised that the mostly Conservative Senate should introduce more government bills and should require Cabinet Ministers to testify personally before its committees. This vision of harmonious relations between the Upper and Lower houses never materialized as the Liberals took over the government in the following year.

In 1951 the Liberal Government Leader, Wishart Robertson, tried again to reform the Senate from within. First, he proposed a special committee to study the directions such reform might take. This committee would base its recommendations on the guidelines of former Prime Minister Mackenzie King who, Robertson maintained, came to believe that reform must come from within the Senate itself. Robertson thought that this study should suggest that the Senate strengthen its committees, focus its legislative review on expenditures, mandate a special committee on one major public issue per year, and separate the positions of Government Leader and Senate Majority Leader.

The latter reform, he explained, would give the Senate greater control over legislative schedules, committee assignments, and allocation of internal resources. In addition to these internal reforms, Robertson urged that some formula be arrived at for maintaining party balance through appointments. At the time, there were only eleven Conservatives in the Senate. Finally, he proposed that senators retire at age seventy-five. Both Liberal and Conservative senators, however, opposed these proposals during five months of debate and forced Robertson to withdraw the motion for a special committee on reform. Like most before him, his attempt at reform had failed.

Robertson's proposals, nevertheless, went on to become the focus of reform movements which did succeed. In 1965, for example, Parliament approved Pearson's proposal that senators retire at seventy-five. In the 1960s and 1970s the Senate strengthened its committees, empowered special committees to investigate major public problems, and gained some control over its internal decision making. Finally, since 1974, Prime Minister Pierre Elliott Trudeau has tried to bring more Progressive Conservatives into the Senate with his ad hoc policy of replacing departing PC senators with fellow party members. We see then that, despite their initial rejection in 1951, several of Robertson's suggestions have been implemented and are established practice today.

Robertson's proposals and the reforms which eventually were adopted required no more than the existing power of the Senate, Parliament, or the Prime Minister to be approved and implemented. Proposals from other sources have called for fundamental changes in Canada's federal system and, therefore, require approval by the provinces. What Canada lacks now is a formula by which both the federal and the provincial political structures might be reformed at the same time.[66] With respect to these concerns about structures, Senate reform has been discussed at two federal-provincial conferences, both of which were called to reframe the constitution.

The first of these conferences took place in 1927. Its delegates, guided by the Liberal federal government, discussed reform only vaguely, as a gesture to Parliament which wanted the provinces' opinions on the issue. Thus, the conference issued no resolutions on the topic. The provinces indicated that they wished above all to eschew an elective Senate. Not until 1969 was the topic raised at another federal-provincial conference.

When Lester Pearson became Prime Minister in 1963, one of his primary goals was to develop a formula whereby the federal and provincial governments together could amend those BNA Act provisions which pertain to federal-provincial matters. While this project was little advanced during Pearson's 1963-68 government, Pierre Elliott Trudeau gave fresh impetus to the issue with a series of federal-provincial conferences from February 1969 to June 1971.

The conferences considered Trudeau's draft for a new Canadian constitution which would supplant the BNA Act. The draft outlined several Senate reforms: (1) the provinces would be more fairly represented (this would especially benefit the western provinces); (2) the provinces would appoint one-half of the senators; (3) the Upper House would have special powers to review federal appointments, official language policies, and human rights legislation; (4) senators would be given limited but renewable terms; and (5) the Senate would have a suspensory rather than an absolute veto.[67]

While these proposals were being discussed in the federal-provincial conferences, they met a storm of protest in the Senate. Senator Daniel A. Lang asserted that the Senate must approve a new constitution, and proposed a special committee to study the question. Lang's motion resulted in the Joint House of Commons–Senate Special Committee on the Constitution (1970-71). This committee evaluated Trudeau's proposals in depth and then put out a report in 1972 which followed their general contours. Because the federal and provincial governments at the Victoria Conference of June 1971 had been unable to agree upon a formula for amendments, however, constitutional reform was postponed indefinitely. In April 1976, Mr. Trudeau resumed his attempts at "patriating" the constitution.

At the constitutional conferences, the optimists predicted that the Senate would become a parliamentary linch-pin for a new federal system. If the provinces appointed half the senators and the Upper House exercised its new powers, in other words, it would be well equipped for a federal-provincial role.[68] What was missing, however, was a formula for constitutional reform, without which the federal government can only implement such modest reforms as procedural changes, which the Senate or Parliament could adopt unilaterally.

In March 1973, Senator David Croll called for debate on several of such procedural changes. These reforms included: (1) a six-month suspensory veto; (2) a limit on the representation of any one party to two-thirds of the Senate's membership; (3) compulsory retirement at age seventy; (4) selection of the Government Leader and the Speaker by senators rather than by the Prime Minister; (5) prohibition of the Government Leader from belonging to the Cabinet; and (6) various reforms of the committee system including compulsory resignation from committee chairmanships at age sixty-five. Although these proposals would have made the Senate more independent and effective, Senator Croll's colleagues generally argued against them. They maintained that these changes would dilute the power of the Senate, dichotomize government and Senate leadership, and discriminate against older senators who are still productive. Senator Croll's debate, thus, did not change the Senate's rules or operations at all.

After Trudeau won the 1974 election he sent word down to the Senate that it must initiate reform from within. Indeed, Trudeau indicated that he would make no further Senate appointments until these changes were under way. On Trudeau's instructions the new Government Leader, Raymond Perrault, solicited suggestions from senators as to what changes they could make. He then discussed the suggestions with a number of high-level officials in the Prime Minister's Office and the Privy Council Office. Despite these efforts, the reform movement died at this stage. For some reason, Senate reform had lost priority, and its momentum dwindled once again.

Although there are many obstacles to Senate reform, two reasons why those in the best position to initiate change in the Senate—the Liberal government and senators—do not press for meaningful reforms are paramount. First, the Liberal government is unwilling to undermine the Upper House which has been theirs since 1943. In other words, it is reluctant to make the Senate independent of government selection of its leaders and control of its activities and resources. Second, Senate business reviewers enjoy power over Senate resources. In other words, they fear that changes in the committee system will cause changes in the allocation of funds to projects. Until these anxieties are overcome, reform efforts such as Croll's or Perrault's will continue to fail, or will be implemented only very gradually as Robertson's was.

THE SENATE, REPRESENTATION, AND DEMOCRATIC THEORY

Except for the New Democratic party MP, Stanley Knowles, few critics believe that the Senate should be abolished altogether. Rather, they say, it is a dying institution which needs new lifeblood. This book will go beyond these conventional critiques to side with Knowles, whose perennial private-member bills call for abolition. I take this stance for two reasons. First, the Senate's role runs counter to the contemporary norms for representation in advanced liberal democracies. Second, attempts at reform have always had excessively long gestation periods and, in the end, have done little to correct imbalances in the Senate's role.

It is an old saw that certain members of a political system command greater attention from decision makers than others do. Yet, such students of liberal democracy as Robert A. Dahl, V. O. Key, Robert E. Lane, and David O. Sears maintain that it is rare for the political elite simply to promote the values and needs of those who have the greatest access. Dahl, for example, holds that even apolitical citizens often hold values and needs in common with the political elite, and thereby share in the decision-making process.[69] Key, as well, suggests that there is an internal restraint among public officeholders which gives them a sense of fair play; thus, they give access to diverse opinion groups.[70] Lane and Sears, finally, maintain that democratic consensus forces political leaders to advocate measures which respond to public opinion to some degree.[71]

Allan Kornberg and Lloyd Musolf are interested in the contribution legislatures make to the growth of democracy; they suggest ways in which legislators can best solve problems in the political system through responsive representation.[72] Legislators, they say, at the very least should provide a link between the ruling elements of a political system and its population, "to obtain necessary information, to provide a catharsis for societal grievances, and to generate support if not enthusiasm for its policies".[73] They say that legislatures in advanced systems could function quite comprehensively according to democratic norms by channelling inter-group conflict, by representing all groups in a society, by enhancing the rule of law, by ratifying and legitimizing public policies, by strengthening the responsive administration of government programs, and by helping to promote national integration and the development of national identity. The above review of the Senate's role shows that Canadian senators do, indeed, perform many of these tasks. Yet, the review also indicates that senators perform their tasks in a way that is antipathetic to democracy.

What is usually at stake in Canadian federal politics? Charles Lindblom's "partisan mutual adjustment" model fits political decision making in the federal arena rather well. While most routine legislation makes incremental and technical changes to existing laws, most non-routine legislation initiates changes in policy by means of business- and finance-oriented bills.[74] Working primarily through the Banking, Trade, and Commerce Committee, senators find ways to influence administrative decisions and the practical provisions of legislation which might affect the business and financial communities. Because many senators are actually directors of corporations and have responsibility for certain aspects of their parties' financial organizations, they often act as key intermediaries between business and government.[75] As such they provide for fellow members of the business elite a preferential access to legislative decision makers and, thus, to the process of decision making itself; they also teach their business associates how to live with government intervention in the marketplace. In this way they contribute to the stabilization of Canada's liberal democracy. Their dual influence parallels that of U.S. lobbyists, as Lewis Anthony

Dexter describes them.[76] A basic difference, however, is that Canadian senators are on the government payroll whereas lobbyists are not. This fact suggests that a major dimension of senatorial behaviour is inconsistent with the norms of liberal democracy. We have already seen that stable relations between business and government are achieved at quite a cost to democracy in Canada. To be sure, senators from the business community are fortunate in being able to hold, simultaneously, corporate and public offices. However, the business community is the only segment of Canadian society which benefits to any significant degree from senators' ability to maintain jointly offices in private and public sectors. For instance, only one senator, Edward M. Lawson, holds a union leadership post.

It is hard to conceive of a liberal democracy in which business does not have easy access to government. In the United States, for example, lobbyists protect business interests by taking advantage of multiple access to Congress which results from the lack of party discipline.[77] Even if we grant, however, that business should have strong relations with government in a liberal democracy, the Canadian Senate violates another major assumption on which Dahl and others tell us a liberal democracy rests: namely, that all segments should have *reasonably equal* opportunities for access to the process of decision making.[78] The domination of the Senate by business leaders clearly militates against equal access.

The remainder of this book performs a twofold task. First, it shows how the Senate violates the tenets of democracy because it is a lobby from within. Second, it sets a scenario for the Senate's abolition.

Chapter 2 looks at senators' ties with various segments of Canadian life. It examines the structure of the Canadian political elite, especially its ties with big business. It shows that senators are often both business and political notables.

Chapter 3 points up how the dual-elite connections of many senators reinforce oligarchic strains in contemporary Canadian politics. Porter, Presthus, and Clement have argued that the Canadian political system gives disproportionate weight to the business viewpoint. Chapter 3 asserts that the Senate serves as a crucial nexus in this current mode of elite accommodation.

Chapter 4 takes a critical look at the institutional consequences of Lester Pearson's and Pierre Trudeau's attempts to reform the Senate. The spurt of social investigation during the late sixties and early seventies notwithstanding, this chapter shows that many reform efforts resulted in only piecemeal or even undesired changes in the bent of the Senate's role, and thereby strengthened the lobby from within. Chapter 5 asks whether appointees can ever really represent the people's interests in democracy. Chapter 6 likewise compares the responsiveness of senators and MPs to various publics within the Canadian system. Taken together, Chapters 5 and 6 show that the appointment process produces mainly senators who represent only a select stratum of society, namely political and business notables.

Chapter 7 calls for the abolition of the Senate only after considering its systemic consequences, as well as obstacles to and a scenario for its accomplishment. It also considers how existing institutions might be strengthened or new ones created to do the job that the Senate was designed for but failed to do; that is, to protect provincial and regional interests; to survey legislation regularly; and to assure that the party with a majority mandate really responds to all of the people.

NOTES

1. Aristotle, *The Politics*, translated by Ernest Barker (New York, 1962), p. 185.
2. Arthur Hailey, *In High Places* (New York, 1962), p. 85.
3. Canadian Institute of Public Opinion Survey, September 16, 1961.
4. Canadian Institute of Public Opinion Survey, December 17, 1964.
5. H. Finer, *Theory and Practice of Modern Government*, revised edition (New York, 1949), p. 400; and A. V. S. Turberville, *The House of Lords in the Age of Reform, 1784-1837* (London, 1958), p. 419.
6. P. A. Bromhead, *The House of Lords and Contemporary Politics: 1911-1957* (London, 1958), p. 12; P. A. Bromhead and Donald Shell, "The Lords and Their House", *Parliamentary Affairs* (Autumn, 1967), pp. 337-49; F. A. Kunz,

The Modern Senate of Canada, 1925-1953: A Re-appraisal (Toronto, 1965), Chapter 1; and Robert A. MacKay, *The Unreformed Senate of Canada* (Toronto, 1963), pp. 9-11.

7. Bromhead and Shell, "The Lords and Their House"; Kunz, *The Modern Senate of Canada*, pp. 17-23; Carl J. Friedrick, *Constitutional Government and Democracy*, revised edition (Boston, 1950), pp. 305-06; and Finer, *Theory and Practice of Modern Government*, p. 409.

8. These are: Canada, Australia, the United States, West Germany, Austria, and Switzerland. The reasoning behind such constitutions is discussed by K. C. Wheare, *Federal Government* (London, 1963), p. 189; Robert A. Dahl, *A Preface to Democratic Theory* (Chicago, 1956), Chapter 3, and *Pluralist Democracy in the United States* (Chicago, 1967); Edward L. Pinney, *Federalism, Bureaucracy, and Party Politics in West Germany* (Chapel Hill, N.C., 1963), Chapter 2.

9. MacKay, *The Unreformed Senate of Canada*, pp. 36-37.

10. *Parliamentary Debates on Confederation of the British North American Provinces* (Quebec, 1865; Ottawa, 1951), p. 29.

11. Ibid., p. 571.

12. Ibid., p. 88.

13. Ibid., p. 36 (emphasis added).

14. Ibid., p. 88.

15. Kunz, *The Modern Senate of Canada*, p. 317.

16. MacKay, *The Unreformed Senate of Canada*, p. 47.

17. Ibid., p. 43.

18. In his introductory words on the proposed Upper House, Macdonald indicates that appointment would be by the regional governments (*Debates on Confederation*, p. 36). Since Brown later asserted that appointment would be by "those holding the confidence of the representatives of the people" (Ibid., p. 88), it appears as if Macdonald's view lost out in the compromise.

19. See MacKay, *The Unreformed Senate of Canada*, pp. 50-54; and R. MacGregor Dawson, *The Government of Canada* (Toronto, 1964), p. 304.

20. Henry S. Albinski, "The Canadian Senate: Politics and the Constitution", *American Political Science Review*, 57 (1963), p. 381. See also MacKay, *The Unreformed Senate of Canada*, p. 62.

21. MacKay, *The Unreformed Senate of Canada*, p. 199; and the author's own tabulations.

22. MacKay, *The Unreformed Senate of Canada*, p. 113.

23. Kunz, *The Modern Senate of Canada*, pp. 316-36.

24. Ibid., p. 294.

25. Ibid., pp. 304-15.

26. Ibid., p. 314.

27. Albinski, "The Canadian Senate: Politics and the Constitution".
28. Richard J. Van Loon and Michael S. Whittington, *The Canadian Political System* (Toronto, 1971), pp. 354, 482.
29. W. L. White, R. H. Wagenberg, and R. C. Nelson, *Introduction to Canadian Politics and Government* (Toronto, 1972), p. 138; Allan Kornberg, *Canadian Legislative Behavior* (New York, 1967), p. 20; and Van Loon and Whittington, *The Canadian Political System*, pp. 482, 489.
30. Van Loon and Whittington, *The Canadian Political System*, p. 482; and White, Wagenberg, and Nelson, *Introduction to Canadian Politics and Government*, p. 138.
31. Peter C. Newman, *Renegade in Power: The Diefenbaker Years* (Toronto, 1963), pp. 97, 112-14, 161, 285, 356, and 374; and *The Distemper of our Times* (Toronto, 1968), pp. 64, 198, 200, and 374.
32. Senators J. J. Connolly, John Nichol, Richard Stanbury, Gildas Molgat, and Bernard Alasdair Graham.
33. F. C. Engelmann and Mildred Schwartz, *Political Parties and the Canadian Social Structure* (Toronto, 1967), p. 122.
34. Ibid., p. 126.
35. K. Z. Paltiel, *Political Party Financing in Canada* (Toronto, 1970), pp. 25-26, 33, and 200.
36. Allan Kornberg, David Falcone, and William Mishler, *Legislatures and Societal Change: The Case of Canada*, Comparative Legislative Studies Series, No. 90-002 (Beverly Hills, 1973), pp. 28-31.
37. Charles Lindblom, *The Intelligence of Democracy* (New York, 1963), pp. 137-38; Gabriel A. Almond and G. Bingham Powell, *Comparative Politics* (Boston, 1966), pp. 61-62, and 108-09.
38. Bruce MacDonald, "Conflict of Interest Issue Looms in Senate's Handling of Bank Bills", *The Globe and Mail* (Toronto), July 7, 1964.
39. "Two Senate Warhorses Give B.C.'s Bennett a Lesson in Politics", *Toronto Daily Star*, July 23, 1964.
40. See Senator L. P. Beaubien, *Debates of the Senate* (May 16, 1972), pp. 343-44; and Senator David Croll, *The Proceedings of the Standing Senate Committee on Banking, Trade and Commerce* (June 14, 1972), pp. 5-8.
41. "Senator Denies Altering Bill to Aid His Firms, Gets Committee Backing", *Toronto Daily Star*, May 19, 1969.
42. Senator Salter Hayden, *Debates of the Senate* (October 8, 1970–March 4, 1971), p. 641.
43. Robert Presthus, "Interest Groups and the Canadian Parliament: Activities, Interaction, Legitimacy and Influence", *Canadian Journal of Political Science*, 4 (December 1971), p. 454.

44. C. E. S. Franks, "The Dilemma of the Standing Committees of the Canadian House of Commons", *Canadian Journal of Political Science*, 4 (December 1971), pp. 467, 470.
45. Anonymous Interview, Ottawa, April 11, 1975.
46. Senator Paul Martin, *Debates of the Senate* (December 17, 1971), pp. 1648-50.
47. Maurice Western, "War of Nerves in Ottawa", *Winnipeg Free Press*, December 15, 1971; Arthur Blakely, "Senators to Pass Tax Bill or May Lose Jobs", *The Gazette* (Montreal), December 16, 1971.
48. Canada, Parliament, Senate, Banking, Trade, and Commerce Committee, Income Tax Bill, *Hearings*, 28th Parl., 3rd sess., December 13, 1971–December 20, 1971.
49. *Debates of the Senate* (May 16, 1973), pp. 584-85.
50. *Debates of the Senate* (December 4 and 12, 1973), especially pp. 1239-40; 1337-38.
51. Canada, Parliament, Senate, Standing Committee on National Finance, *Growth, Employment and Price Stability*, 28th Parl., 3rd sess., 1971.
52. Canada, Parliament, Senate, Standing Committee on National Finance, *Information Canada*, 29th Parl., 2nd sess., April 1974.
53. Figures provided by a student, Frank Ortino.
54. Kunz, *The Modern Senate of Canada*, p. 267.
55. Canada, Parliament, Senate, Honourable David Croll, *Report on Action on the Recommendations of the Special Committee on Aging*, 30th Parl., 1st sess., October 22, 1974.
56. Canada, Parliament, Senate, Special Committee on Poverty, *Poverty in Canada*, 28th Parl., 3rd sess., 1971.
57. Interview, Ottawa, April 22, 1975.
58. Canada, Parliament, Senate, Special Committee on Science Policy, *A Science Policy for Canada*, 1 (1970), 2 (1971), 3 (1973).
59. Anonymous Interview, Ottawa, April 11, 1975; and Peter Aucoin and Richard French, "The Ministry of State for Science and Technology", *Canadian Public Administration*, 17 (Fall, 1974), p. 464.
60. Canada, Parliament, Senate, Special Committee on Mass Media, *The Uncertain Mirror*, 28th Parl., 3rd sess., 1970.
61. Ibid., pp. 157-68; Isaiah Litvak and Christopher J. Maude, "Interest Group Tactics and Foreign Investment", *Canadian Journal of Political Science*, 7 (December 1974), pp. 616-29.
62. See Newman, *The Distemper of Our Times*, pp. 224-26; and Litvak and Maude, "Interest Group Tactics and Foreign Investment", especially p. 724.
63. Ian Adams *et al.*, *The Real Poverty Report* (Edmonton, 1971).

64. E. Russell Hopkins, *Confederation at the Crossroads* (Toronto, 1968), p. 315.
65. Albinski, "The Canadian Senate: Politics and the Constitution", pp. 378-91.
66. J. Peter Meekison, "Constitutional Reform in Canada", in J. Peter Meekison (ed.), *Canadian Federalism: Myth or Reality* (Toronto, 1971), pp. 235-52.
67. Pierre Elliott Trudeau, *The Constitution and the People of Canada* (Ottawa, 1969), pp. 28-34.
68. E. Donald Briggs explains this view and contests it in "Federalism and Reform of the Senate: A Commentary on Recent Government Proposals", *Queen's Quarterly*, 78 (Spring, 1970), pp. 56-71.
69. Robert A. Dahl, "The Polyarchy Model", in Norman R. Luttbeg (ed.), *Public Opinion and Public Policy* (Homewood, Ill., 1968), p. 209.
70. V. O. Key, Jr., *Public Opinion and American Democracy* (New York, 1963), p. 539.
71. Robert E. Lane and David O. Sears, *Public Opinion* (Englewood Cliffs, N.J., 1964), p. 49.
72. Allan Kornberg and Lloyd D. Musolf, "On Legislatures in Developmental Perspective", in Allan Kornberg and Lloyd D. Musolf (eds.), *Legislatures in Developmental Perspective* (Durham, N.C., 1970), pp. 26-30.
73. Ibid., p. 28.
74. Kornberg, Falcone, and Mishler, *Legislatures and Societal Change.*
75. Engelmann and Schwartz, *Political Parties and the Canadian Social Structure*, p. 126; and Paltiel, *Political Party Financing in Canada.*
76. Lewis Anthony Dexter, *How Organizations are Represented in Washington* (New York, 1969), pp. 103, 130.
77. Morton Grodzins, "American Political Parties and the American System", in Aaron Wildavsky (ed.), *American Federalism in Perspective* (Boston, 1967), p. 137.
78. Peter Bachrach, *The Theory of Democratic Elitism: A Critique* (Boston, 1967), pp. 88-92; and Robert A. Dahl, "Power, Pluralism and Democracy: A Modest Proposal", a paper delivered at the 1964 annual meeting of the American Political Science Association, Chicago, September 9-12, 1964.

2. Senators' Standing Among the Canadian Elite

In Canada members of the business elite find it relatively easy to win political positions, just as members of the political elite find it easy to win positions in the business world.[1] Very often they become leaders in both elite circles. This is especially true of Canadian senators.

THE BUSINESS AND POLITICAL ELITE

Wallace Clement has done the most recent study of Canada's business elite and its ties with the political elite.[2] Clement defines the business elite as the directors and senior executives of Canada's 113 dominant corporations. He surveyed the backgrounds of 775 members of this elite and found they come mostly from families which are upper-class, central Canadian, and British or French. Very few who are neither British nor French, he found, rise this high in the business world. The business elite, moreover, is 85 per cent university educated; many of its members, indeed, did their undergraduate work at the University of Toronto, or McGill, and their graduate work at Harvard.

Clement's study reveals how often Canada's business elite is also linked to Canada's political elite. First, at private institutes which attempt to bring the elite from several sectors together to exchange views on matters of mutual concern, the business elite usually forms the largest contingent. These institutes include the Canadian Executive Service Overseas, the Canadian-American Committee, the Ontario Research Foundation, and the illustrious Institute for Public Policy Research. Second, 163 members of the business elite say that they are active in a political party. Only two, however, say they were members of the Social Credit party; and none identified themselves as belonging to the New Democratic party. Third, over 39 per cent of the business elite are friends or relatives of the political elite. Many are members of the political elite themselves, and serve in the Senate, or on government boards or commissions. They thus maintain membership in both elite circles.

Clement's findings convey how closely "high background" is related to membership in Canada's business elite and, in turn, in the political elite. Many senators, as members of both elite groups, benefit doubly from special status within the system. The remainder of this chapter looks at this phenomenon from three standpoints: (1) how often the Prime Minister appoints members of the business elite to the Senate; (2) the political and socio-economic backgrounds of senators, including the political environments that they represent; (3) the behavioural and institutional orientations that senators bring to their work.

BIASES OF THE APPOINTMENT PROCESS

The fact that the Prime Minister appoints all senators clearly provides a selection of incumbents with similar socio-economic backgrounds. The Prime Minister, of course, must limit his personal preferences to some degree.[3] First, he must fill vacancies according to the seats allotted each province. Then, in some cases, he must select persons from regions within provinces which "traditionally" have a member, and must also appease religious and ethnic groups with at least some representation. Finally, he must limit his choices to those who are thirty years of age or over and possess $4,000 of debt-free real property. After these various constraints are taken into consideration, for the most part the Prime Minister has a free hand in appointing senators from the socio-economic and political groups he prefers.

There is a considerable amount of lobbying for Senate seats. The available data on Pierre Elliott Trudeau's appointees from 1968 to 1974 indicate that candidates have to work hard to become senators.[4] With the exception of Prince Edward Island

and Newfoundland, Senate vacancies which have developed during the Trudeau government have generated much competition. As a result of this competition, aspirants from Alberta and Manitoba had only one chance in eleven of being appointed; on the average, only 23 per cent of all aspirants on file in the Prime Minister's Office (PMO) ever win Senate seats. While some aspirants wage public campaigns, most spend their time and energy cultivating friends in strategic party or government positions. Over half of the Trudeau appointees (seventeen out of thirty-two) won their seats with the help of Cabinet contacts alone. Many of the remaining appointees had obtained letters from non-Cabinet officeholders, or partisan associations. Such extra-Cabinet input, then, does influence the appointment of senators.

Aspirants for the Senate, moreover, achieved success more often if those who nominated them cited their party loyalty or their service in public offices. Forty per cent of the former nominees won seats in the years 1968 to 1974; 60 per cent of the latter group of nominees, moreover, were likewise appointed during the same years. This constitutes favouritism; and it reflects the degree to which Prime Ministers care well for fellow party workers and politicians. In addition to these biases, aspirants whom referees believe represent business often win seats in the Senate. Indeed, 38 per cent of aspirants recommended for their standing in the business community won appointments during our time period.

Two additional phenomena illustrate the bias and favouritism that determine most appointments. Aspirants who were recommended because they represent ethnic groups or geographic portions of provinces seldom won seats. Only 11 and 8 per cent, respectively, of such nominees actually won appointments. Thus, although it is difficult to become a senator, partisan, political, and business notables recorded relatively high success rates in their bids for an appointment.

With respect to Trudeau's appointments, bias appears to be as much a sin of omission as of commission. That is, Trudeau simply chooses to let certain seats remain empty so as to keep his options open and wait for the optimal appointment from a political standpoint. In November 1976, for example, 18 of the 104 Senate seats remained vacant, even though three years earlier (July 1973) the Prime Minister's Office had detailed knowledge of several groups and political parties in Canadian society which were underrepresented in the Senate. By province, they were—

British Columbia: the interior of the province; the New Democratic (NDP) and Progressive Conservative (PC) parties

Alberta (with two vacancies as of November 1976): German Canadians; PCs; women; southern Alberta (Lethbridge)

Saskatchewan (with two vacancies): NDPs and PCs; women

Manitoba (with one vacancy): NDPs; women; northern Manitoba

Ontario (with four vacancies): NDPs; Italian Canadians

Quebec (with four vacancies): Irish Catholics; the Quebec City and Trois Rivières regions; Social Credits

New Brunswick (with two vacancies): Acadians

Nova Scotia (with one vacancy): Acadians

Newfoundland: PCs

Despite the large number of Senate seats which have remained vacant, Trudeau often ignores lacunae for long periods of time. From July 1973 to November 1976 he appointed Senators Louis-J. Robichaud (New Brunswick) and Ernest George Cottreau (Nova Scotia) to fill Acadian vacancies in their respective provinces and Senator George Isaac Smith to strengthen the PC delegation from Nova Scotia. During the same period, however, he appointed senators from Quebec, New Brunswick, and British Columbia who in no way compensate for the underrepresentation of various groups. In fact, he appointed two senators in direct violation of the PMO's list of the most pressing needs. Jack Austin is one. A Vancouver businessman who had served as the Principal Secretary to the Prime Minister, he was appointed to the Senate although he represented neither non-Liberals nor residents of B.C.'s interior. Maurice Riel was another. A Montreal lawyer and Liberal fund raiser, he won his seat although he did not represent Quebec's Irish Catholics, the Social Credit party, Quebec City, or Trois Rivières.

Thus we see how the Prime Minister weaves the political, socio-economic, and geographic texture of the Senate. First, he can, if he chooses, ignore vacancies and demographic gaps in provincial delegations. Second, he can choose senators according to very rigid standards. In Trudeau's case, these standards have worked in favour of Liberal party operatives, public officeholders, and notables in the business community.

SENATORS' BACKGROUNDS

Political Environment

Since this chapter is concerned primarily with the overlapping membership of senators in the business and political elite, it is essential to consider the political environment that they currently represent as part of their background. One crucial relationship supports this assertion. Of the twenty-five senators who held directorships in 1975, twenty came from either Ontario or Quebec and sixteen lived in either Toronto or Montreal.[5] Since these cities are the financial capitals of Canada, senators who live there can collect directorships much more easily than can their colleagues from the "hinterlands". This finding underlines the importance to this study of a profile of senators from the standpoint of the political divisions in which they reside. The profile centres on "constituency" and province characteristics of the seventy-one senators whom this author interviewed personally. For the purposes of comparison, this section presents as well "constituency" and province background data for 189 MPs whom Allan Kornberg and William Mishler interviewed concurrently with this study.

"Constituency"

Senators are appointed. Nonetheless, senators from Quebec do have at least nominal responsibility for representing specific constituencies and several other senators attempt to represent specific districts within their province.

Elections need not be the only link between representatives

and constituents. Thus, we might expect that senators who come from urban and competitive centres would probably be attuned to a type of public demand different from the kind of request made to senators from rural areas, no matter how they got into office.[6] Liberal senators from areas with predominantly Progressive Conservative MPs (for example, Alberta, which has only one Liberal MP) might assume extensive representational functions because the area's disproportionately large opposition delegation in the elected House of Commons has only very limited influence on the Liberal government. The likelihood is that at least some senators establish close representational ties with an area in their province. The federal constituency within which they reside thus will serve as a surrogate "constituency" in this profile of the political environments from which senators come.

From the many possible components of political environment at the constituency level, this profile focuses on eleven factors. Three of these factors pertain to the social diversity of the constituencies—"population"; "number of ethnic groups which are represented in large numbers in a constituency"; and "per cent of population urban". Eight concern the political environment of the ridings during the 1968 federal election (the one preceding the time of the interviews)—the per cent of voter turnout; the per cent of the vote won by each party; the degree to which support for various parties is close to equal;[7] and the difference between votes drawn by the winning and second strongest parties in the senators' "constituencies".

Compared with MPs, senators are relatively urban creatures. (See Appendix II: *"Constituency".*) Senators also seem to come disproportionately from areas which, in the 1968 election, were strongly Liberal and weakly NDP. Members of the Upper House, finally, live in more competitive ridings than MPs.

Province

If Prewitt and Eulau are correct in their assertion that legislators from urban and competitive areas receive more pluralistic demands than other legislators, then, presumably, senators from relatively urban provinces which foster intense competition for House of Commons seats would notice the conflicting pressures emanating from these provinces and competing for their attention. Likewise, senators from provinces which are underrepresented in the Upper House would become a focus for certain types of pressure if their provinces' Liberal delegations in the House were small or nonexistent. A province's political environment is more than simply a geographic region which a senator is appointed to represent. Rather, it is also a social and political space which influences the way a senator perceives and performs his roles.

With respect to the political environments from which senators and MPs come, the following large differences emerge from comparing the data (see Appendix II):[8] (1) senators come from somewhat less populous provinces than MPs. The average senator's province has 3,120,000 inhabitants, while the average MP's has 4,489,000. (2) The average senator's province is 57 per cent urban, while the average MP's is 61 per cent urban. We saw above that the constituencies in which senators reside are more urban than those of MPs. The figures suggest then that senators are drawn disproportionately from urban ridings even if they represent relatively rural provinces. (3) Senators' provinces receive a greater proportion of representation in the Upper House than they do in the House of Commons; MPs' provinces receive about the same proportion of representation in both houses. The average senator's province has a 1.3 to 1 ratio of Senate to Commons seats, while the average MP's province has a 1 to 1 ratio. These three differences all stem from the fact that the Atlantic provinces, which are relatively underpopulated, are overrepresented in the Senate.

Socio-economic and Political Backgrounds

Looking at the socio-economic and political backgrounds of senators, one finds that private and public careers blend in fascinating ways. This observation applies equally to those involved as both business reviewers and social investigators (Chapter 1). Space does not allow detailed background profiles of all senators. It must suffice to trace a few profiles which point out the relation between background and legislative orientation particularly well.

For instance, *Salter Hayden* (b. 1896), the business reviewer *par excellence*, comes from a relatively modest background. His father, an Irish Catholic, was a civil servant in Ottawa. Hayden received his education at the University of Ottawa which was then a small Catholic college. Growing up in a political town, Hayden developed his love of Parliament at an early age. As a youth he sat for hours in the House of Commons gallery, dreaming about being a great parliamentarian.

Hayden never did win a seat in the House of Commons. He ran in 1935 and was defeated. Distinguished, none the less, as a party worker, he was summoned to the Senate in 1940, where he has excelled as chairman of the Banking, Trade, and Commerce Committee. Hayden's real fame, however, is as a top corporation lawyer with McCarthy and McCarthy, one of Toronto's most prestigious law firms. He has also been on the board of directors of several corporations, including the Bank of Nova Scotia, Union Carbide (Canada Ltd.), and Atlantic Sugar Refineries. The young Salter Hayden perhaps never dreamed that he could reach the top in two worlds, the parliamentary and the corporate. Yet now he epitomizes success in both sectors.

Alan Macnaughton (b. 1903), currently Banking's deputy-chairman, brings to his work a blend of parliamentary and business success every bit as strong as Hayden's. Macnaughton received a much more prestigious education than did Hayden; he attended Upper Canada College, McGill University, the London School of Economics, and the University of London. Also, during his career as an MP (1953-66), Macnaughton held several important positions—which included being chairman of the Public Accounts Committee and the Liberal party caucus, as well as Speaker of the House of Commons. Thus, even before he came to the Senate in 1966, Macnaughton had had a distinguished parliamentary career.

The standing Macnaughton had in Parliament when he became a senator, he lacked in the business community. He soon made up this deficiency, however, by piecing together one of the longest lists of corporate positions held by members of the Upper House. These positions include the chairmanship of two boards, the presidency of four firms, and directorships in twelve companies. Macnaughton typifies those senators who are able to parlay the right social and business connections and standing in the political community into a chain of corporate ties.

A slightly less typical product of political and corporate life is *Ernest Manning* (b. 1908), the former Premier of Alberta. Raised in a small Saskatchewan town, Manning trained to become a Baptist minister in Calgary. He did not, however, attend an accredited college or attain a baccalaureate degree.

Manning, in fact, received his education on the job. During the 1930s, he was chief disciple and heir apparent to Alberta's Social Credit Premier, William Aberhart. In this position, he wielded considerable power in the party which wrestled with what was seen as the mid-depression financial hammerlock of Toronto's "Bay Street". Manning succeeded Aberhart in 1943 as Premier, in which position he worked for twenty-five years to promote the massive financial and industrial growth in Alberta which was based on significant oil finds in the late 1940s. He left the office in 1968.

The events which turned Alberta from an agricultural hinterland into a financial and resource-industry power transformed Manning as well. Indeed, the Ernest Manning of today bears little resemblance to the thin, self-effacing, right-hand man of Aberhart who preached the populist gospel of Social Credit. Manning, now the political sophisticate, has, since his 1970 appointment to the Upper House, accumulated a string of directorships which rivals that of all but a handful of Bay Street lawyers. He currently sits on the boards of six corporations, including the Canadian Imperial Bank of Commerce, the Manufacturers' Life Insurance Company, and the Steel Company of Canada. Manning's status among the nation's business elite notwithstanding, he has yet to "arrive" in the Senate. He belongs only to the ancillary business review committee, National Finance.

The socio-economic and political backgrounds of social investigators in the Senate often contrast sharply with those of business reviewers. The career of Senator *David Croll* (b.

1900) exemplifies these differences. His family came to Canada from Russia in 1905. Croll grew up in Windsor. He was admitted to the Bar at the age of twenty-five. At the same time, he was beginning a political career which would see a mercurial rise. He was Mayor of Windsor by age thirty (1930), and an Ontario MPP and Cabinet Minister at thirty-four. His appointment to the Ontario Cabinet, in fact, marked the first time that a Jew had risen to such political heights in Canada. In 1937, however, the Liberal Premier, Mitch Hepburn, fired Croll from the Cabinet for siding with labour in the notorious General Motors strike in Oshawa.

Croll was never again to receive a Cabinet post, provincial or federal. In 1945 he ran for the House of Commons and won. Croll took the abrasive tack of criticizing his own party, in and out of caucus, while in the House of Commons. Knowing that he was viewed as a firebrand by Liberal leadership, and therefore probably would not be called to the Cabinet, he accepted a 1955 Senate appointment from Prime Minister Louis St. Laurent—again, a pioneer in a public office previously closed to Jews. In the Upper House, Croll could pursue his social policy interests with much less embarrassment to the Liberals. Chapter 1 details his achievements as a social investigator.

As a senator, Croll has served intermittently on the Senate Banking Committee, often haranguing its members to declare conflicts of interest when they arise. Croll has meanwhile continued his life in business and law; he practices corporate law in Toronto, and is chairman of the boards of City Savings and Trust Company, and of the First City Financial Corporation Limited.

Senator *Keith Davey* (b. 1926), is a social investigator who has distinguished himself by chairing the Senate's special study of the mass media. Raised in Toronto, Davey came from a United Church, middle-income family. He attended a free public high school, North Toronto Collegiate (rather than the expensive and exclusive Upper Canada College). He then went on to Victoria College, University of Toronto (instead of the more "establishment" Trinity College).

After university, Davey entered the advertising business.

When not on the job, he devoted an immense amount of his time to organizing for the Liberal party. Known as "the Rainmaker", because pundits have noticed that his high profile in the Ottawa scene usually signals another election, Davey has directed the 1962, '63, '65, and '74 federal campaigns for his party. If one includes two minority governments, he claims a three-for-four success rate.

In reward for his loyal party work, Davey received a Senate seat in 1965. From this base he has been able to work on his main policy interest, mass media. Davey believed that the Canadian media, because of the monopolistic practices of the owners, and the funnelling of millions of dollars of Canadian advertising money into U.S.-controlled media, was not serving the public and the interests of the country. As we have seen, Davey's Special Committee on Mass Media proposed a number of measures which have been adopted by the governments responsible and by the media. They should materially improve the media's accountability and Canadian content.

Earl Hastings (b. 1924), also a social investigator, grew up in Regina, Saskatchewan, where he attended Regina College and Success Business College. Moving to Calgary in the midfifties, he worked as a petroleum landman. Hastings then began to work within the Liberal party's Alberta organization. First, he served as president of the provincial Liberal Association (1961-62); then he ran, without success, for the House of Commons in 1962 and 1963. Summoned to the Senate three years later (1966), Hastings became active as a social investigator, particularly on Croll's poverty study. He has also done volunteer work with prisoners at the federal penitentiary in Drumheller, Alberta.

It was no particular surprise, then, when Hastings began outspokenly to press for reform during a 1972 parole system study, conducted by the Legal and Constitutional Affairs Committee. He did raise eyebrows, however, when he brought federal prisoners to Ottawa to testify in support of his proposals. As we saw in Chapter 1, he was successful in his reform attempts.

The parole system study put Hastings into the Senate limelight, and gained the attention of Prime Minister Trudeau, who, until the defection of Jack Horner to the Liberals, relied on Hastings to be the government's spokesman in Alberta. To many Albertans, Hastings became the best link to the federal Liberal caucus and ultimately to the Prime Minister. Thus, the residents of Banff National Park in Alberta petitioned Trudeau in 1976 to appoint Hastings as the Cabinet Minister for the province.

These individual profiles suggest that the socio-economic and political orientations of Senate business reviewers differ significantly from those of social investigators. The three business reviewers, we saw, all eventually became successful businessmen, while the three social investigators have had less distinguished, even marginal, careers in business. A subsequent chapter will look much more thoroughly into the relationships between senators' backgrounds and their preferences for either business review or social investigation. The following sections, however, study their socio-economic and political backgrounds in more detail, and compare them with the backgrounds of other elites in Canada and elsewhere. How, then, do senators compare with other elites in terms of age, the length of time that they have lived in their region of the country, urban upbringing, education, religion, ethnic origin and occupation, and political careers?

Socio-economic Characteristics

Age is an important social characteristic. Several authors assert that age strongly influences how a legislator sees and performs his role, inasmuch as older legislators are less ambitious and less responsive to the public than younger ones.[9] From 1925-63 the average age of Canadian senators was sixty-nine.[10] Since then the average age has dropped considerably because the 1965 law required senators to retire at age seventy-five. Among the senators whom this author interviewed, the average age was sixty-two years, with a range from forty-one to eighty-six. (See Appendix II: *Social Background.*) The cut-off line was not seventy-five because members appointed before 1966 had the option of retiring or staying on. By way of contrast, among the

189 MPs whom Kornberg and Mishler interviewed, the average age was fifty. U.S. Congressmen in recent years likewise have averaged around fifty years of age.[11] In the elective U.S. Senate from 1947-57, Donald Matthews found that the average age was in the mid-fifties.[12] Thus, the Canadian appointive system provides members for the Upper House who are relatively aged, even for "senators".

In Anglo-American systems law is the profession most highly represented in legislatures.[13] Lawyers, more than any other professional group, have a combination of the requisite skills and the freedom from forty-hour-a-week jobs needed by legislators. In the U.S. Senate and House of Representatives, for instance, the proportion of lawyers often exceeds 50 per cent.[14] Their predominance in Canada's Parliament is less extreme. Only 34 per cent of Canadian senators and 33 per cent of MPs are lawyers.

Kenneth Prewitt maintains that, after lawyers, businessmen are the most highly represented profession in Anglo-American legislatures.[15] Indeed, 27 per cent of our 71 senators gave "businessman" as their occupation. Kornberg and Mishler found that 26 per cent of their 189 MPs were "businessmen".

Whether or not they call themselves "businessmen", senators hold a much larger number of directorships in Canada's principal corporations than MPs do. Thirty-nine per cent of the senators held directorships, while only 6 per cent of the MPs held places on boards.[16] The senators filled, altogether, 219 positions whereas the MPs occupied only 34.

Educational backgrounds and parentage are characteristics which John Porter and other scholars have looked at closely when studying social status. Porter says that Canada's social elite is composed of those educated British (English, Scottish, and Irish) Protestants whose ancestry dates at least one generation back in Canada.[17] This group, he says, controls the major economic, social, and political institutions in Canadian society.

Senators are somewhat less well educated than MPs. In the sample, 72 per cent of the senators had some university education, while 77 per cent of Kornberg's and Mishler's MPs did. These findings might reflect the difference between generations whereby older senators probably had fewer opportunities to go to university. Senators ventured considerably less than MPS out of their native provinces to receive part of their education (the figures, respectively, are 27 and 42 per cent); they did, however, travel slightly more than MPS to schools outside of Canada (17 and 16 per cent, respectively).

Between 1925 and 1963, 54 per cent of senators were Protestant,[18] while 57 per cent of the senators interviewed for the present study are Protestant (the comparable figure among Kornberg's and Mishler's MPS is 50 per cent). Well over half of the interviewed senators are of British descent; 63 per cent claim totally British parentage. Kornberg and Mishler, on the other hand, found that only 46 per cent of their MPS have both British fathers and mothers. A very small 6 per cent of senators have two parents who belong to neither of Porter's two ethnic "charter groups" (British or French); the comparable figure for the MPS is a relatively large 26 per cent.

Finally, where a legislator was raised might affect his view of his roles. For instance, legislators raised in small towns would be aware of problems connected with rural life that legislators raised in cities would have no direct experience of. Senators, in contrast to the Kornberg and Mishler MPS, are overwhelmingly city cats. Fifty-four per cent were raised in cities (for MPS the figure is 35 per cent). With respect to the length of residence in the various provinces, legislators who have spent most of their lives in the province they represent would, presumably, have specific loyalties which would affect their view of their work. The data indicate that considerably more senators than MPS have spent most of their lives in the Atlantic provinces. We will see in a later chapter how this continuity of residence among Atlantic-provinces senators relates to their views of their work.

Political Careers

Because of the ideological stances that parties potentially demand of their members,[19] party affiliation could influence senators' views of their roles. A Prime Minister very rarely offers Senate appointments to persons who are not members of his party. The two longest-tenured members among the interviewed senators are Liberals. Both were appointed in 1940 by the Liberal Prime Minister, Mackenzie King. Since 1940 Progressive Conservatives have formed the government for only a six-year period, 1957 to 1963. There are only fifteen PCs among the seventy-one interviewees.

A more serious inequity which results from appointments is the fact that the small parties are rarely represented. Among the seventy-one senators, in fact, only Ernest Manning represents a minor party (the Social Credits). The election system usually assures a more equitable party distribution in the House of Commons. In the 1971 federal election, the New Democratic and Social Credit parties won 6 and 4 per cent, respectively, of the seats in the House of Commons.

Did many of our senators have political careers before their appointments? This is an important question, for their previous public and party offices could well affect their legislative roles. Experienced public officeholders, presumably, know better than newcomers how to influence legislation. Fifty-three per cent of the interviewed senators held previous public office; whereas as many as 69 per cent of Kunz's senators (1925-63)[20] and as few as 37 per cent of MPs (1930-65) did.[21] (See Appendix II: *Political Background.*) The interviewed senators' former offices, moreover, were prestigious ones: 31 per cent had been MPs; 18 per cent had served in provincial legislatures. Canadian senators, therefore, surpass MPs in previous political experience; in addition, they surpass American senators, the most experienced legislators in the United States, as well.[22]

Besides having served for several years in public office, legislators may have gained valuable political experience in party offices. Sixty-five per cent of the senators, as compared to 62 per cent of Kornberg's and Mishler's MPs, had held party offices on some level. Indeed, 32 per cent of the Senate respondents had been members of their party's national executive. These figures are impressive when compared to those pertaining to legislators in other Western systems. In the United Kingdom, for example, only 21 per cent of Conservative and Labour candidates for the House of Commons had ever held a party office.[23] Only 9 per cent of U.S. Congressmen, moreover, reported holding positions in their party's national executive.[24] Again, Canadian senators prove to be among the most politically experienced legislators in the world.

Experience in the Senate itself might also affect the way a member views his role in the legislative process. It takes a senator some time to learn the ropes in the Upper House and to acquire the necessary standing to have a real impact on his colleagues and on legislation. The sample indicates that, since 1966 when compulsory retirement at seventy-five became law, the average tenure of senators (sixteen years) has actually dropped—by almost one-half—to 8.32 years.[25] Because of the relatively high turnover rate of MPs, the figures for senators' tenure, however, compare favourably with the corresponding figures for Kornberg's and Mishler's MPs (MPs' average tenure is 7.23 years).

SENATORS' ORIENTATIONS

Senators' background experiences have, presumably, had an impact on their orientations towards politics and the institutions in which and with which they must work. A person with several years' experience in the business world, for instance, will probably bring to the Senate motives and institutional views that differ markedly from those of a political operative who has spent most of his time organizing for a party. To analyse senators' identities within the context of the Canadian political elite, therefore, we must consider their behavioural and institutional orientations. The former pertain to senators' motives for being in politics and choosing particular legislative tasks; the latter concern the relationships they have with the people and groups whom they represent, and with their political parties. Whenever possible, this profile of senators' orientations will draw, for purposes of comparison, from data on Canadian MPs and legislators elsewhere.

Behavioural Orientations

Although Harold Lasswell years ago pointed up the value of studying "personality-like"[26] influences on politics, to this day very few studies have looked at legislators' personalities to explain why they choose particular legislative roles. Some students of legislators' roles, however, have mentioned the importance of behavioural orientations in explaining role perceptions;[27] this section expands on those rare studies which actually employ empirical analysis of legislators' personalities.[28]

The interviews posed several questions specifically designed to uncover senators' motives for various types of behaviour in the political arena. The questions asked them: why they got into politics; the most important things they have tried to accomplish as senators; why they have remained in the Upper House; why they chose their specialities and their favourite committees; why they suggested certain revisions of bills; why, most commonly, they contact Cabinet Ministers; and whether they consider themselves full-time legislators.

The majority of senators, 54 per cent, as compared to 41 per cent of Kornberg's and Mishler's MPs, say that they first got into politics because of personal experiences such as family involvement or friendships during their youth. (See Appendix II: *Behavioural Orientations.*) Thirty-four and 24 per cent, respectively, of the senators attribute their political activity to partisan and altruistic motives (e.g., "to provide good legislation for the country", or "to help the little guy"). Interestingly, only 11 per cent of the MPs say that they are in politics for altruistic reasons whereas 59 per cent cite partisan motives. We should keep in mind, however, that senators, by virtue of their immense experience in politics, often have risen to the position of "statesmen", and therefore we should not be surprised to find that a greater proportion of senators than MPs choose altruistic ways of describing their motives.

Eighty-nine per cent of the senators believe that their most important job as legislators is to influence policy. This compares favourably with the 81 per cent of MPs who have the same orientation. When asked why they stay in the Upper House, 51 per cent of the senators say that they like the political influence that goes with the job, and 48 per cent say that they receive personal gratification from the *esprit de corps* and ritual of the Senate. Fifty-six per cent of the MPs cite the latter reason for staying in the House of Commons, as well; but a surprisingly smaller proportion (33 per cent) say that they stay because they enjoy a feeling of political efficacy there. Senators, however, are somewhat less inclined than MPs to see themselves as full-time legislators (61 *versus* 72 per cent).

Senators much less often than MPs report contacting Cabinet Ministers about constituency matters involving governmental services (14 as opposed to 71 per cent). As we might expect from the proportion who see themselves as policy-influentials, 45 per cent of the senators say that they contact Cabinet Ministers because of policy concerns, while the figure for MPs is 43 per cent. Many senators (44 per cent) say that they chose their specialities because they enjoy contributing their occupational expertise, especially their "good business sense", to the policy process; altruistic motives or political experience are only secondary influences on the development of their skills in particular types of legislative review. When asked why they have pressed for specific revisions to legislation, however, 49 per cent of the senators recall altruistic motives while only 20 per cent cite occupational expertise. Again we find that, perhaps because of their political experience and standing in Canadian society, senators like to give the impression of being good statesmen who serve their country by lending their considerable occupational expertise and a fair measure of altruism to policy considerations.

Institutional Orientations

Social scientists who analyse politics in terms of structure and function often look to institutions to explain why politicians think and act the way they do. Indeed, Harold Lasswell calls institutions "practices by which values are shaped and destined".[29] He and many other scholars say that politicians think and act in terms of the standard operating procedures for relations with institutions.[30] For instance, a legislator might cherish above all the need for party discipline, and therefore take on or reject certain tasks on the basis of what he thinks his party's leaders expect of him. On the other hand, the same legislator might believe that interest groups simply grind axes without providing useful information and, as a result, he might automatically reject requests for appointments from lobbyists. Our knowledge about such orientations among legislators demands that some attention be given to senators' views of their relationships to the institutions with which they interact. Such analysis might reveal that these relationships influence senators' choice of legislative roles.

Heinz Eulau and John Wahlke are two "structural-functionalists" who have applied the concept to the study of legislators.[31] Wahlke, especially, underlined the concept of "office" and how its institutional nature shapes legislators' expectations concerning role perceptions and performances.[32] The following portion of this chapter will look at the institutional orientations of senators in two ways. First, it will ascertain if senators go to their party for information on bills and how accountable they feel to their party. Second, it will determine how members view their relations with extra-party institutions. In this regard, two questions merit attention. First, does the fact that they are appointed to represent a particular province affect senators' orientations? Second, do senators try to find out what the people of their province and interest groups think about major issues before Parliament?

Senators and Parties

Conventional wisdom has it that senators are relatively independent of party ties.[33] Since they are appointed, their tenure, unlike that of MPs, does not depend upon partisan support in exchange for party endorsement and assistance during campaigns for re-election. The fact is that, whether or not they are thought to be independent, senators rarely give up party loyalties. When voting, they seldom cross party lines. Partisanship is often as intense in the Senate as it is in the House of Commons.[34]

In the interviews, two questions got the senators talking about how they viewed their parties as institutions in the legislative arena. The first presented senators with a list of party and extra-party sources and asked them to state which sources offered good advice and information about the opinions people in their province hold concerning legislation before Parliament; the second asked senators to select two sources that consistently provide accurate information. Fifty-four per cent called party sources "at least reliable", while 23 per cent identified their party as one of the two outstanding sources. (See Appendix II: *Institutional Orientations.*) Seventy and 39 per cent of Kornberg's and Mishler's MPs, on the other hand, rated party sources, respectively, as "reliable" and "outstanding". An additive variable combines senators' responses to these questions (Variable 7, "rates party sources highly for advice").

A later item in the questionnaire gave senators a list and asked them to select those persons and organizations on it to which they feel somewhat accountable or highly accountable for what they do. Fifty-two per cent said that they felt somewhat accountable to party leaders or organizations, while only 9 per cent said that they felt most accountable to these two groups. Comparable figures for MPs were 64 per cent and a much higher 27 per cent. A variable which combines the two types of responses among senators measures the intensity of their party loyalty (Variable 8, "feels accountable to party").

Senators and "Constituents"

In order to ascertain whether senators feel an obligation towards the provinces that they represent, the interview posed two questions. The first was: "What are the most important things you want to accomplish as a senator?" Senators' responses were coded, first, according to whether they said their chief legislative purpose was to provide services for the people of their province. Only 11 per cent considered provincial service to be most important. This is exactly the same proportion Kornberg and Mishler record for their MPs. (See Appendix II: *Institutional Orientations.*) Second, only 6 per cent of all senators who reported that they spend most of their time on legislative policy, rather than on representation of their province, mentioned issues which concerned a particular province; one senator, in addition, focused on an issue which concerned a lesser area within his province. MPs, in this regard, reveal much stronger orientations to provincial and local policy issues (23 and 20 per cent, respectively). Similar data from the U.S. indicate that Canadian legislators of both houses put much less emphasis on localized representation than American legislators do. In Roger Davidson's study of U.S. Congressmen, 82 per cent of the respondents described themselves as "tribunes"—those who reflect the needs of a regional constituency; while 17 per cent described themselves as "brokers"—mediators between parochial and general interests.[35] Using the same categories, Wahlke and his colleagues found the respective proportions among the members of four U.S. state legislatures to be 52 and 32 per cent.[36] It is ironic, however, that Canadian senators, whose legislature was originally established to provide representation for the provinces, should actually reveal less of a tendency towards localized representation than MPs.

The data, then, probably disclose the pervasive influence of appointment by the Prime Minister on senators' representational orientations. Obviously, they tend to think in terms of national representation. In other words, when they do see themselves as mediators between Canada's people and national decision-making mechanisms, senators tend to formulate their roles in the broadest terms. They say on their questionnaires that they "represent" by "bringing the business perspective to politics", "protecting against too much government involvement in the marketplace", or "bringing about social reforms". Since they owe their seats to a national political figure, the Prime Minister, and do not have to satisfy the folks back home to keep their seats, it is not surprising that they focus their attention on the big, national issues.

Communication with Ad Hoc and Attentive Publics

To what extent do representatives respond to the pressures of public opinion? Kenneth Prewitt and Heinz Eulau maintain that "responsive" legislators are more inclined than others to consult attentive publics (that is, clearly defined political interest clusters), or ad hoc pressure and opinion groups (that is, groups which form and act in response to specific issues).[37] Responsive legislators, in other words, are those who attempt to gather and organize opinions from structured sources, i.e., attentive publics and ad hoc groups, rather than who simply make decisions based on their own ideas of what the public wants or on ideas they obtain casually from acquaintances and "the man in the street".

The interviews posed several questions to find if and how senators respond to ad hoc and attentive publics. One of these asked if members try to find out how the people whom they represent feel about the issues before Parliament. The overwhelming majority say "yes" (82 per cent as compared with 90 per cent in the MP study). (See Appendix II: *Institutional Orientations.*) Fifty-eight per cent say the sources they consult for advice on legislative issues are structured (for MPs the figure is 74 per cent). A follow-up question asked senators to evaluate the reliability of the various sources. Sixty-two per cent of the senators call structured groups the "most accurate" of all available sources of information. This figure contrasts sharply with the relatively small 28 per cent of MPs who call structured sources "the most accurate". Senators' responses to this question were added so that members who call structured sources "reliable" received one point and those who call them "the most accurate" received two points (Variable 5).

The list of persons and organizations to which senators feel accountable included the names of several ad hoc and attentive publics. Seventy-five per cent of the senators claim some accountability to those structured sources while 57 per cent report that they are most accountable to them. The respective figures for MPs are 66 and 38 per cent. Senators, thus, again prove themselves to be more attuned to these structured sources than are MPs. Variable 6 combines the two indicators in an effort to measure the intensity of senators' views. Senators probably respond to extra-party structures more often than MPs do because they are less beholden to their parties, even though they seldom break party lines when voting.

Variable 9 (Appendix II) probes the *expansiveness* of senators' loyalties. They receive points each time they say that they seek out and consider the opinions of newspaper editorials, party organizations, business, labour, or religious groups; or each time they claim that they are accountable to their parties, the people of their province, the residents of an area in their province, or all Canadians. Even by this standard, senators appear to be somewhat more responsive than MPs to a fairly wide range of structures (average score for senators, 4.46; for MPs, 3.92).

Although senators tend more than MPs to see themselves as responsive to external influences, outsiders seem to contact them less than they contact MPs. Forty-nine per cent of senators as opposed to 78 per cent of MPs receive what they term a "large" amount of mail; 75 per cent compared to 92 per cent frequently receive phone calls or personal visits. Senators say that their communication from constituents concerns policy questions more often than MPs do (66 per cent *versus* 50 among MPs). Their perceptions of whether such communication concerns service requests (70 per cent) and comes from a cross-section of the publics that they represent (89 per cent) corresponds fairly well with the views of MPs (75 and 92 per cent, respectively).

In sum, senators' institutional orientations differ in several important ways from those of MPs. Senators see themselves as relatively immune to pressures from their parties. They also focus much less often than MPs on regional and local rather than national issues. Their appointment to office notwithstanding, senators are surprisingly open to interest and subgroups' advice and information. They report, however, less actual interaction with these sources than MPs do. Senators' institutional orientations, much like their behavioural orientations, leave the impression that they see themselves as statesmen. They are concerned with the big, national issues. Although they are not closed to outsiders, their particularistic ties are less well developed than are those of MPs.

CONCLUSIONS

This chapter has focused on the privileged position of senators as legislators. Many are endowed with high standing within two crucial elite groups in Canada, the political and the business communities.

Although senators are not the only members of the Canadian elite who have high standing in politics and business, they embody the clearest institutional ways in which the two are connected. First, the process by which senators are appointed strongly favours selection of individuals who have, or show high promise of having, success in both fields of endeavour. Second, senators' ties in both communities tend to intensify if they reside in large urban centres, particularly in Toronto or Montreal. Profiles of the political environments that they represent indicate that senators come most frequently from the more populous areas within their provinces. Third, senators' relatively extensive political and business experience distinguishes them most sharply from MPs. In contrast to MPs, senators frequently sit on corporation boards and have previously won high public and party offices. This fact suggests the degree to which senators' past and present positions link them, institutionally, much more firmly to both business and politics than MPs' positions do. Finally, with respect to their behavioural and institutional orientations, senators, more consistently than MPs, see themselves as statesmen. That is, they are more likely than MPs to describe themselves as legislative specialists whose primary obligation is to bring occupational expertise to the policy-making process rather than to serve their party or their "constituents".

This chapter has pointed up how extensively senators in personal and institutional ways combine the "best" of two worlds. Because of their very high standing in politics and business, they describe themselves as statesmen who give generously of their time to make sure that legislation is as good as possible. In reality, however, their statesmanship works most effectively on behalf of the nation's business interests. We will see in the next chapter how some senators perform their main legislative role, business review, in order to promote the business community's interests and to increase and maintain their personal influence. We will also examine the means employed by the business reviewers' rivals in the Senate, the social investigators.

NOTES

1. John Porter, *The Vertical Mosaic: An Analysis of Social Class and Power in Canada* (Toronto, 1965); Wallace Clement, *The Canadian Corporate Elite: An Analysis of Economic Power* (Toronto, 1975).
2. Clement, *The Canadian Corporate Elite*, pp. 221, 259-65.
3. F. A. Kunz, *The Modern Senate of Canada, 1925-1963: A Re-appraisal* (Toronto, 1965), Chapter 1.
4. These data were provided by Michael Kirby and Michel Rochon of the Prime Minister's Office. They derive from a detailed review of the files of the Director of Nominations. The data cover Mr. Trudeau's government up to and including 1974.
5. *Financial Post Directory of Directors* (Toronto, 1975).
6. Kenneth Prewitt and Heinz Eulau, "Political Matrix and Political Representation: Prolegomenon to a New Departure From an Old Problem", *American Political Science Review*, 63 (June 1969), p. 428.
7. The assumption of this model is that, where perfect competition exists, each party receives an equal number of votes. The author calculated the index by following a modified version of the Rae-Taylor "fragmentation" index. See Harold D. Clarke, Richard G. Price, and Robert Krause, "Constituency Service Among Canadian Provincial Legislators: Basic Findings and a Test of Three Hypotheses", *Canadian Journal of Political Science*, 8 (December 1975), pp. 527-28.
8. With respect to provincial political environment, the profile employs ten variables. Two variables, "population" and "per cent of population which is urban", measure how populous and urban a senator's province is. Five variables determine how well senators' provinces are represented in Ottawa. These are: "number of Senators in 1971", "ratio of the per cent of Senate seats and the per cent of House of Commons seats", and the "proportion of representation as compared to population in (a) Parliament, (b) the House of Commons and (c) the Senate". Four measures delineate the characteristics of political competition in members' provinces. These are: "near perfect competition between parties in per cent of votes"; "per cent of seats won" in the 1968 federal election (the author applied the Rae-Taylor formula to the macro-level by substituting the respective statistics, votes, and seats won, from the 1968 election viewed as a province-wide phenomenon); and "Senator's party is in a favourable competitive position in terms of (a) per cent of votes, and (b) per cent of seats won". With respect to the latter two variables, the party with the greatest percentage of votes or seats in a province was

ascertained. Winning parties received "plus" scores because the votes or seats of the second strongest party were subtracted from those obtained by the winning party. All other parties' scores were derived by subtracting the percentage of votes they won from that obtained by the strongest party. Thus, senators' parties were in a strong competitive position in their province if they received a high "plus" score and in a weak competitive position if they obtained a low "minus" score (e.g., for the latter, "—35" as opposed to "—1").

9. Kenneth Prewitt, *The Recruitment of Political Leaders: A Study of Citizen-Politicians* (Indianapolis, 1970), p. 188; and Joseph A. Schlesinger, *Ambition and Politics* (Chicago, 1966), Chapter 9.

10. Kunz, *The Modern Senate of Canada*, pp. 70-71.

11. T. Richard Witmer, "The Aging of the House", *Political Science Quarterly*, 79 (December 1964), pp. 526-41. See also Roger H. Davidson, *The Role of the Congressman* (New York, 1969), pp. 61-62.

12. Donald R. Matthews, *U.S. Senators and Their World* (New York, 1960), pp. 13-14.

13. William B. Quant, *The Comparative Study of Political Elites*, Comparative Politics Series, 1 (Beverly Hills, 1970), p. 192; Prewitt, *The Recruitment of Political Leaders*, pp. 156-59; Heinz Eulau and John D. Sprague, *Lawyers in Politics* (Indianapolis, 1964), p. 11; Donald R. Matthews, *The Social Background of Decision Makers* (Garden City, N.Y., 1954); and Joseph Schlesinger, "Lawyers and American Politics: A Clarified View", *Midwest Journal of Political Science*, 1 (May 1957), p. 31.

14. Matthews, *U.S. Senators*, p. 33. During the period from 1947 to 1957, about half the U.S. senators had legal training. Over 60 per cent of Davidson's sample of U.S. representatives studied law, *The Role of the Congressman*, p. 37.

15. Prewitt, *The Recruitment of Political Leaders*, p. 159.

16. Data taken from the *Financial Post Directory of Directors* (Toronto, 1970).

17. Porter, *The Vertical Mosaic*, pp. 71, 91, 266, and 386-98.

18. Kunz, *The Modern Senate of Canada*, p. 69.

19. See, for instance, sections of Allan Kornberg's *Canadian Legislative Behavior* (New York, 1967), Chapter 7.

20. Kunz, *The Modern Senate of Canada*, p. 62.

21. Allan Kornberg, "Parliament in Canadian Society", in Allan Kornberg and Lloyd D. Musolf (eds.), *Legislatures in Developmental Perspective* (Durham, N.C., 1970), p. 118.

22. See Matthews, *U.S. Senators*, p. 55; and Schlesinger, *Ambition and Politics*, p. 92.

23. Austin Ranney, *Pathways to Parliament* (Madison, Wis., 1967), pp. 108-98.
24. Davidson, *The Role of the Congressman*, p. 50.
25. Kunz, *The Modern Senate of Canada*, p. 71.
26. Harold D. Lasswell, *Psychopathology and Politics* (Chicago, 1930), Chapter 4.
27. John C. Wahlke *et al.*, *The Legislative System* (New York, 1962), p. 21; and Malcolm E. Jewell, "Attitudinal Determinants of Legislative Behavior: The Utility of Role Analysis", in Kornberg and Musolf, *Legislatures in Developmental Perspective*, p. 478.
28. Schlesinger, *Ambition and Politics*; James David Barber, *The Lawmakers: Recruitment and Adaptation to Legislative Life* (New Haven, Conn., 1965); Kenneth Prewitt, "Political Ambitions, Volunteerism, and Electoral Accountability", *American Political Science Review*, 64 (March 1970), pp. 144-59.
29. Harold D. Lasswell, "World Organization and Society", in Daniel Lerner and H. D. Lasswell (eds.), *The Policy Sciences* (Stanford, Calif., 1951), p. 102.
30. See Amitai Etzioni, *The Active Society* (New York, 1968), pp. 65-68; and Graham T. Allison, "Conceptual Models and the Cuban Missile Crisis", *American Political Science Review*, 63 (September 1969), p. 702.
31. Heinz Eulau, *Micro-Macro Political Analysis* (Chicago, 1969), pp. 100-01, and Wahlke, *The Legislative System*, p. 20.
32. Wahlke, *The Legislative System*, pp. 21-23.
33. Kunz, *The Modern Senate of Canada*, Chapter 4.
34. Henry S. Albinski, "The Canadian Senate: Politics and the Constitution", *American Political Science Review*, 57 (1963), pp. 378-91.
35. Davidson, *The Role of the Congressman*, p. 80.
36. Wahlke, *The Legislative System*, p. 259.
37. Prewitt and Eulau, "Political Matrix and Political Representation", p. 430.

3. Senators and the Politics of Elite Accommodation

"Elite accommodation" is the "style" the Canadian political elite uses to resolve disputes, and to facilitate the policy-making process. Senators, as we will see, adopt the style to serve the corporate world by influencing government from within. We saw in Chapter 1 how business-oriented review of legislation affects the policy-making process. In this chapter we will take a close look at senators who perceive business review as their legislative role; we will also see the ways in which they act out these perceptions and how other policymakers evaluate their impact on the process. Also in this chapter we will look at senators who prefer social investigation as their legislative role, observing how they proceed and whether their work is having an impact.

Robert Dahl maintains that all sectors of society must have reasonably equal access to the process of political decision making if liberal democracy is to thrive.[1] Dahl even proposes a new name for such democracies: polyarchies. Polyarchies, he says, provide universal suffrage, whereby all may participate at least minimally in the decision-making process, and open and free discussion of issues whereby all have access both to available information and to deliberations. In this sort of democracy, no single sector would control the political process.

Many Canadian scholars doubt that such an ideal situation obtains in Canada today, mainly because Canada's political system is built not upon one society but upon several. The multiplicity of these societies derives, as John Meisel points out, from the extensive ethnic and regional divisions in the country which deprive Canadians of a "genuinely shared set of

symbols, heroes, historical incidents, enemies, or even ambitions".[2] We do not have to look far for examples to support
Meisel's observations. The 1976 victory of the separatist party
in Quebec is one; another is the separatist rumblings in the
western provinces that accompanied the Parti Québécois
victory.

How does this fragmentation affect Canada's liberal democracy? S. J. R. Noel's answer to this question has become a
classic statement in Canadian political science.[3] He believes
that such fragmentation precludes the possibility that all segments of Canadian society will achieve equal access to decision
making through open participation and expression of viewpoints. Instead of fulfilling Dahl's criteria, that is, the country
follows a "consociational" model, which modifies the requirements of polyarchy in two important ways. First, the rank-and-
file of such sub-cultures as French Canada see elections as a
less than direct means of obtaining proper representation in
Ottawa. That is, within sub-cultures voters frequently choose
the federal candidate for MP whose party is most likely to
include in the Cabinet several articulate spokesmen of their
groups. As a result, voters within sub-cultures often do not
give much thought to whether the candidates for whom they
vote will be the best representatives of their riding in the House
of Commons. We have already seen (Chapter 1) that voters in
some provinces and regions also feel that a provincial government of a different party from the government party in Ottawa
—which consequently takes strong provincial-rights stances
—can represent their interests better than the MPs that they
send to the House of Commons. Second, when the members
of the elite of various sub-cultures, provinces, and regions
resolve disputes they usually do so in secret. The federal
Cabinet and federal-provincial conferences make most of the
crucial policy decisions in Canada's federal system of government. Deliberations in both bodies are closed to public scrutiny.

Keeping these two Canadian modifications of liberal
democracy in mind, we see why Noel asserts that our system
attains democracy more through elite accommodation than
through relatively equal access to policy decisions. The rank-

and-file of sub-cultures and regional groups often have perceptions of only indirect links to the federal government either through the Cabinet or through a provincial-rights oriented provincial government. In addition, they frequently find themselves in the dark about the process whereby crucial decisions were reached. One clear difficulty arises, however, if we accept elite accommodation as an adequate mode of resolving disputes among segments of Canadian society. The elite tends to extend its influence beyond the resolution of disputes between ethnic groups and regions to conflicts between other sectors. Behind-the-scenes accommodation becomes the norm rather than the exception in the resolution of all sorts of political disputes. The numbing effect of this process on democratic participation probably explains why many Canadians, as we saw in Chapter 1, accept uncritically their appointive Senate, in which members who retain leadership positions in the business world use their legislature as a base for lobbying.

In Chapter 2 we saw that Wallace Clement found considerable overlap in personnel among the elites of various sectors of society. For instance, the same corporate elite directs both the media and business communities, although the two are functionally distinct.[4] The links between the business and political worlds are not as direct. Yet Clement provides ample evidence that official and informal contacts between the two give the business community the greatest access to government.[5]

How does such access occur and how does elite accommodation influence the process? Robert Presthus provides some answers.[6] In his *Elite Accommodation in Canadian Politics*, he shows us exactly how the elite-accommodation style is used to resolve disputes between sectors of the economy. He finds that accommodation between economic groups, rather than occurring in parliamentary debate and study of legislation, mostly takes place behind the scenes. Further, much of the bargaining excludes legislators other than Cabinet Ministers.

Presthus bases these assertions on his findings about how interest groups influence the federal government. In sharp contrast with U.S. lobbyists, he found that interest groups in

Canada register their substantive claims most often with bureaucrats.[7] Yet the group leaders say that Cabinet Ministers are their prime targets, if they can contact them; and that government backbenchers and opposition MPs rank relatively low in group leaders' priorities for lobbying.[8] Only 30 per cent of the leaders ever contact non-Cabinet MPs.[9] More important, Presthus's respondents indicate that a pecking order exists among groups that dictates whether they will concentrate their appeals at Cabinet or MP level. This pecking order places business at the top; thus business gains relatively easy access to the Cabinet, while labour often must appeal to MPs.[10] Presthus's findings suggest that because the Cabinet and the bureaucracy make most policy decisions the business community benefits most clearly from the elite style of accommodation. The following section shows how senators promote business interests even further when such primary access fails to win the day.

SENATORS AS LOBBYISTS FROM WITHIN

Chapter 1 discussed business review in the Senate, and demonstrated the extent to which business reviewers can influence legislation. It pointed out, for example, that the Senate has had considerable impact upon the Investment Companies Act, the Income Tax Act, and the Foreign Investments Act. To what do its members attribute their success? Salter Hayden, Chairman of the Senate's Banking, Trade, and Commerce Committee, gives, as we saw, a very simple explanation of how senators successfully perform business review. These tactics comprise the essential components of lobbying from within. First, senators hear grievances from the business community members who feel that civil servants and Cabinet Ministers have ignored them. Then, senators astutely wield their corporate reputations through the powerful Banking Committee to persuade the department in charge of a bill that certain "technical" changes must be made within it. If the department's Minister finds the case convincing, he will arrange for the government to sponsor amendments which would accommodate the senators' concerns. Cumulatively, "technical" changes often water down such bills, and this result is the aim of lobbying from within. With the help of senators, in other words, business has been able to get its main points across to the government.

Do many senators actually involve themselves in this sort of lobbying, or is it simply Hayden's influence which delivers the ultimate result? This section will ascertain just how widely senators participate in the process. First, the section will show how senators, during the interviews, described their involvement in business review. Second, it will analyse these descriptions statistically, and study them both in the light of senators' actual participation in Senate proceedings and with respect to other members of the Ottawa elite's evaluations of their roles.

The interviews posed four questions to the seventy-one senators to ascertain how they see their legislative roles. These questions were: (1) "Is there any particular work of the Senate in which you consider yourself an 'expert'?" (2) "To which committees do you belong?" (3) "Which two committees interest you the most?" and (4) "Have you personally ever advocated specific revisions of certain legislation?" Taken together, their responses provide an excellent profile of many senators' principal legislative interests. The senators submitted to these interviews on condition that their anonymity be preserved.

One Montreal senator admits without hesitation that he maintains close contact with the corporate world. In addition, he calls himself an expert on business legislation and says he devotes most of his time to work in the Banking Committee. He does not say that he personally has been responsible for specific changes to measures. He has, however, "been involved in a lot of discussions in Banking, Trade and Commerce which over the years have made business legislation much more sound."

Two corporation lawyers in the Senate amplify particularly well the business reviewers' approach. The first says that the main contribution these senators make to the legislative process is an appreciation of the Canadian political system. The federal government, he believes, runs mainly on the goodwill of the business community, and senators are the only ones in Ottawa who really understand this: "Without us the Cabinet and the bureaucracy would never get the type of cooperation out of the private sector which is needed to make the system run." The second corporation lawyer emphasizes the tactics which business reviewers employ. He says that they frequently ask members of their law firms to help them draft amendments to bills. Then they lobby according to an established pattern: "I go to the Minister in charge and show him what I think should be changed in the bill and ask for his cooperation; then I go over to the Commons and start lobbying among the MPs, pointing out, of course, that I have been to see the Minister and that I have his blessing."

Another senator touches upon some of these points when he summarizes his perception of business review. Although the role emerges from the business and legal expertise of senators, he says, it relates most fundamentally to an appreciation of the legislative process. Bureaucrats want to "cover the waterfront" in legislation. Senators, on the other hand, ask two crucial questions of each bill before they vote on it. First, does it preserve Parliament's ultimate authority to make law, especially by denying Ministers excessive discretionary powers? Second, does it meet those requirements of the business community which are essential to maintenance of the free enterprise system? This senator's view, then, is explicitly oligarchic. In fact, he voluntarily suggests that the Founding Fathers established the Senate because "they were worried about the possibility, without an Upper House, of popular swings which would take command in the House of Commons and generate legislation that throws the whole system out of whack." Yet, with respect to tactics, the senator offers a warning to colleagues who think that they can accomplish these oligarchic objectives purely by "influence".

Don't fool yourself about how much you can accomplish by simply going to the Minister and influencing him. The main thing that you have to do is work diligently in Banking, Trade and Commerce and argue your case articulately on the floor of the Senate. That's ultimately what wins the day in the Department. You have to work from the sound base of your reputation. Learn the ropes in Ottawa. Gradually, you will get somewhere.

The interview, participation, and elite-evaluation data on senators' involvement in business review allow us to test statistically the above view of how lobbying from within works. Senators who see themselves as business reviewers, we might expect, most often receive mention from elites in Ottawa because of their involvement in the role. Their chances of being mentioned, however, increase if they follow their business review perceptions through by participating in related Senate debates and committee work.

Measures of Involvement in Business Review

As a measure of their *perceptions* of involvement in the role, senators were classified as business reviewers if they (1) said that their speciality was commerce or finance; (2) belonged to the Banking, Trade, and Commerce or the National Finance committees; (3) named one or both of these committees as among their favourite assignments; or (4) reported specific revisions which they had advocated for bills concerning commercial or financial legislation. Table 3.1 reveals that 21 per cent of the senators said that they specialize in business review; 49 per cent said that they belonged to either the Banking or Finance committees; 41 per cent considered at least one of these two to be their favourite committee; and 25 per cent referred to specific instances where they had advocated revisions of business or financial legislation. By comparison, Allan Kornberg and William Mishler interviewed 189 MPs and came up with 16, 22, and 23 per cent for the first three categories.[11]

Because multiple indicators were available to measure senators' involvement in business review, we can more easily ascertain the *degree* to which the legislators perceive themselves as playing the role. Factor analysis[12] was used to see whether the correlations of responses to the indicators are such that an additive variable is appropriate in this case. The results of the test argue very strongly for an additive variable,

Table 3.1 BUSINESS REVIEW IS HIGHLY IDENTIFIABLE IN THE CORRELATION OF SENATORS' VIEWS OF THEIR LEGISLATIVE ROLES

Type of Involvement	% Involved		Correlation of Types of Involvement Among Senators				Factor Loadings*	Factor Scores
	Senators	MPs	1	2	3	4		
1. Speciality is Business Review	21	16	1	.52	.62	.49	.67	.12
2. Belongs to committee which concerns Business Review	49	22		1	.84	.53	.87	.25
3. Favourite committee concerns Business Review	41	23			1	.50	.92	.57
4. Suggestions for revisions have concerned Business Review	25	Not asked				1	.61	.13
	n=71	n=189				Eigenvalue (% of variance explained)	2.43 (100)	

*Unrotated

as the four types of involvement load on one factor which explains 100 per cent of the variance among the items.[13] Senators obtained twelve points if their speciality was business review, twenty-five points if they belonged to either the Banking or the Finance committees, fifty-seven if they indicated that one of the two committees was their favourite, and thirteen points if they advocated revisions of pertinent bills. The average senator received forty-one points on the index.[14]

Two measures ascertain senators' *participation* in business review. These consist of: (1) the number of pages *Debates of the Senate* gave to speeches individual senators made on business matters; and (2) their attendance records on the Banking, Trade, and Commerce and the National Finance committees. The measures cover senators' participation for a year prior to the interviews. On the average, senators spoke for 3.25 pages about business-related matters;[15] and they attended 3.25 meetings of the Banking and/or Finance committees.[16]

This interviewer asked 609 members of the Ottawa political, bureaucratic, and media elite, in person or by mail, to name those senators that they considered to be particularly effective as legislators; and then to explain why they had named the senators they did. The respondents came from four groups: senators, non-Cabinet MPs, top-level civil servants, and members of the parliamentary Press Gallery. Since senators were asked this question personally, they responded with greater frequency (100 per cent) than did non-senators (32 per cent). Individual civil servants, whose response rate was the greatest of the non-senators (38 per cent), named fewer senators than did the other three groups.[17]

Senators received points for effectiveness in business review only if this reason was explicitly mentioned by the Ottawa elite. Respondents usually gave more than one reason for a nomination. Among these were: "knows the right people in Ottawa" (20 per cent); "has served long and well in public life" (38 per cent); and "works effectively in his party organization" (16 per cent). As it turned out, 38 per cent of those senators that the Ottawa elite considered to be effective legislators were cited for work related to business review. The

Figure 3.1 Senators who perceive roles in business review and participate in related deliberations are the most likely to be mentioned for the role by the Ottawa elite

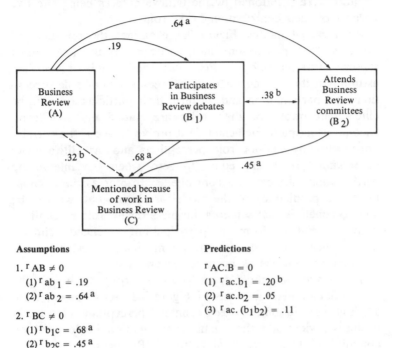

Assumptions	Predictions
1. $^r AB \neq 0$	$^r AC.B = 0$
(1) $^r ab_1 = .19$	(1) $^r ac.b_1 = .20$ [b]
(2) $^r ab_2 = .64$ [a]	(2) $^r ac.b_2 = .05$
2. $^r BC \neq 0$	(3) $^r ac.(b_1 b_2) = .11$
(1) $^r b_1c = .68$ [a]	
(2) $^r b_2c = .45$ [a]	

[a] significant at .001 level   [b] significant at .01 level

average senator received 1.41 nominations for this reason.[18]

Interrelatedness of Business Review Role Perceptions,
Participation, and Elite Views of Influence

Having delineated senators' legislative role perceptions, participation in parliamentary deliberations, and effectiveness according to other members of the Ottawa elite, we may now look at the interrelatedness of these variables. In Figure 3.1, "Business Review" measures senators' orientations towards business review; "Participates in Business Review debates" and "committees" are constructs which represent members' overt participation in this form of legislative work; "Mentioned because of work in Business Review" represents the number of times senators were mentioned by the Ottawa elite as being effective because of their contribution to the role.

As a causal model, Figure 3.1 examines the relevance of senators' role perceptions and participation in two distinct senses.[19] First, employing Pearson's coefficient,[20] it tests the assumption that the correlations between senators' role perceptions and participation and, in turn, their participation and the elite's perceptions of their roles are statistically significant. Second, using path coefficients,[21] it probes to see if the correlations between senators' role perceptions and the elite's views of senators' roles are equal to zero when the intervening participation variables are controlled.[22] Insofar as the assumptions and predictions of the model are borne out, we will be able to conclude that senators' business review role perceptions trigger specialized forms of participation in related deliberations which, in turn—as intervening factors—establish the senators' reputations as business reviewers.

The results of the causal analysis strongly support the assumptions and predictions of Figure 3.1. As assumed, there are high correlations between senators' perceptions of roles in business review and their actual participation in debates and committees. The correlation between "Business Review" and "Attends Business Review committees", in fact, is extremely strong (0.65, $p < 0.001$). Also, as assumed, senators' participation in debates and business review committees correlates well with the Ottawa elite's perceptions of a role in business review ($p < 0.001$ for both coefficients). With respect to the model's predictions, the findings strongly support the expectation that "Attends Business Review committees" is an intervening factor (path coefficient = 0.05); they indicate, as well, that "Participates in Business Review debates" is not a strong intervening influence (path coefficient = 0.20, $p < 0.01$). These results make sense. Since most business review is done in committees, senators who follow through on their preference for the role would have to devote considerable time to committee work in this field.

This causal analysis substantially supports senators' perceptions of their business review roles. That is, the findings lend credence to senators' claims that in their roles they actually influence legislation, for the findings show that the Ottawa elite often mentioned senators as being effective legislators because of their involvement in the role. Furthermore, with respect to senators' practice of "business review", the results corroborate what we already had heard from one of the outstanding business reviewers. It is not sufficient for a senator to cast himself in the role; he must also participate fully in related deliberations to become effective and to attract the attention of the Ottawa elite. Business review influences legislation most, then, when a senator fully utilizes the resources available to him as a legislator, especially the Banking or Finance committees. The successful business reviewer recognizes the potential power of his senatorial prerogatives. Full utilization of these institutionalized resources is the essence of lobbying from within.

SOCIAL INVESTIGATION AS AN EMERGING ROLE

Chapter 1 described social investigation as the Senate's emerging role of real importance. Under the auspices of special committees, we saw that Senators Maurice Lamontagne, David Croll, and Keith Davey all conducted special studies which have had a great impact on the field of social legislation. Such an impact often has rivalled that of business reviewers on business legislation. The chapter also suggested that resourceful social investigators follow three essential steps: (1) they carve out a policy speciality in keeping with their interests and talents; (2) they marshal support to study their policy area in a special committee or investigation and they generate as much input as possible from like-minded citizens; (3) they press the Liberal caucus and Cabinet Ministers to respond affirmatively to the study's findings. When answering interview questions concerning their specialities, their committee work, and their proposals for legislative revisions, senators indicate that these three techniques are always at work.

One senator who has been quite active on the Science Policy Committee attributes his initial interest to his "eclectic personality". With respect to science, he says, he has always been "a reasonably informed outsider". He has studied science on his own for some years now, particularly as it relates to changes in political and social values. The Science Committee provides an excellent opportunity for him "to stand at the crossroads of science, politics and society". Even U.S. Congressmen have complimented him on his fine work in the committee, stating that its hearings and reports provide the best source of information available on the role of science in the "post-industrial era". Not satisfied with such compliments, the senator tries to see that the government does not pigeonhole the committee's work. He has spoken out in several forums about the need for a comprehensive science policy, especially one that would permit Canada to reap fully the technological benefits of research. Indeed, since he joined the committee, he has spoken at eighteen universities in an effort to get his view across to academics and students.

A senator who has been very active on the Poverty Committee believes he became interested in the study because of his social origins and his constituency background: he grew up in a poor family and now represents a depressed section of his province. While an MP, his origins also sparked his interest in two legislative fields, veterans' affairs and fisheries. As a senator he does an immense amount of "case work" for poor "constituents". In fact, he reports a heavier load of mail from the people in his province than any other senator. Claiming intimate knowledge of current social programs, he finds that the Poverty Committee is the perfect forum in which to register his dissatisfaction with inequities in the system. The committee's study and report, in addition, have given him ammunition for making points in the Liberal caucus about the inadequacies of social programs.

A senator on the Mass Media Committee traces his interest in the work to his concern about newspaper monopolies. He believes that they dominate his province economically and politically. He has, thus, waged a personal crusade against them for a number of years. The report of the media committee gives him clout with the department which must prosecute such cases, Consumer and Corporate Affairs. In addition to the monopoly problem, he has followed through on several other concerns which were registered in the report. Working alongside him has been Senator Keith Davey, who, the senator noted, can sidestep caucus and the Commons, and take "their" appeals directly to the Prime Minister and "two or three key Ministers".

From interview, participation, and elite evaluation data, we might expect that senators who call themselves dedicated social investigators attract attention from the Ottawa elite. We might expect as well that senators who participate in relevant deliberations would likewise attract such attention.

Measurement of Involvement in Social Investigation

To evaluate senators' reports of involvement in social investigation, a number of factor analyses were performed in an attempt to ascertain which types of legislative work, other than business review, formed a cluster. Social-cultural legislative specialities were considered "social investigation". These included welfare, housing, media, or ethnic relations. The committee assignments or preferences which corresponded to these specialities were Health, Welfare, and Science; Mass Media; or Poverty. Limiting the social investigation committees to these four would of course exclude, *a priori*, many types of legislative involvement which social investigators might find interesting.

Some preliminary factor analyses, thus, attempted to relate involvement in social-cultural legislation, as ascertained by members' specialities and committee work, to similar activities in the fields of foreign affairs, legal and constitutional affairs, and socio-economic resources (e.g., labour or environment). Only senators' work in the latter legislative field related well to their various activities in the social-cultural area. Senators were classified as involved in the socio-economic resource field if their specialities related to the environment and conservation, fisheries, agriculture, labour, and science policy, or if they belonged to or chose as their favourite assignment either the Science Policy or the Transportation and Communication committee.

Since social investigation is usually conducted on an ad hoc basis in the Upper House, i.e., in special committees or studies, it is imperative that the measure of the intensity of senators' involvement in the role be related to the legislative involvement of MPS. Presumably, MPS investigate social problems in a more regularized way than do senators. For instance, MPS can study social problems in any of twelve standing committees.[23] Because this MP data extends our view of how social investigation is performed in Parliament as a whole, it is included in the factor analysis.

The distributions of senators' and MPS' responses (Table 3.2) indicate that, under all but one category of activity (2.a), MPS are considerably more intensely involved in social investigation than are senators. Factor analysis of senators' and MPS' responses finds that the construct "social investigation" accounts for 60 per cent of the variance in the types of involvement that the legislators report.[24] Thus, the additive variable "social investigation" should be highly reputable as a measure. Table 3.2 ("Factor Scores") lists the points assigned to senators for various types of involvement in social investigation. The average senator received thirty-seven points.[25]

To ascertain how much social investigators play out their roles and how great an influence they have on legislation, an analysis was conducted of senators' speeches and committee attendance in the year previous to the interviews, and of the reasons members of the elite gave for nominating them. On the average, senators took up 6.69 pages of *Debates of the Senate* with discussions of social problems;[26] they attended 3.21 meetings of committees whose work centres mainly on social investigation;[27] and they received 3.23 nominations from the political elite for their work in social investigation.[28]

Social Investigation Role Perceptions, Participation, and Elite Views of Influence

A causal model (Figure 3.2) assesses how greatly social investigators' role perceptions influence their participation in related deliberations and, in turn, how their participation ultimately influences legislation as assessed by the Ottawa elite. We find that "Social Investigation" does relate very well with

Table 3.2 SOCIAL INVESTIGATION RELATES TO PARLIAMENT'S REVIEW OF LEGISLATION WHICH CONCERNS SOCIAL, CULTURAL, AND RESOURCE MATTERS

Type of Involvement	% Involved		Correlation of Types of Involvement Among Senators and MPs						Factor Loadings*	Factor Scores
	Senators	MPs	1	2	3	4	5	6		
1. Speciality										
a. Social-cultural concerns	17	23	1	.25	.13	.07	.31	.15	.32	.10
b. Resources, socio-economic	9	37		1	.11	.30	.06	.43	.44	.12
2. Belongs to committee										
a. Social-cultural concerns	44	42			1	.33	.54	.28	.55	.20
b. Resources, socio-economic	44	52				1	.17	.68	.70	.28
3. Favourite committee										
a. Social-cultural concerns	18	30					1	.19	.55	.23
b. Resources, socio-economic	23	50						1	.78	.42
	n=71	n=189							2.00	
								Eigenvalue (% of variance explained)	(60)	

*Unrotated

Figure 3.2 Senators who perceive roles in social investigation and participate in related deliberations are the most likely to be mentioned for the role by the Ottawa elite

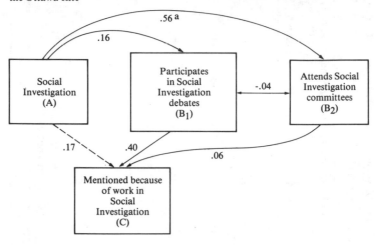

Assumptions

1. $r\,AB \neq 0$

  (1) $r\,ab_1 = .16$

  (2) $r\,ab_2 = .56$ [a]

2. $r\,BC \neq 0$

  (1) $r\,b_1c = .40$ [a]

  (2) $r\,b_2c = .06$

Predictions

$r\,AC.B = 0$

  (1) $r\,ac.b_1 = .10$

  (2) $r\,ac.b_2 = .19$

  (3) $r\,ac.(b_1 b_2) = .09$

[b] significant at .001 level

"Attends Social Investigation committees" (correlation coefficient = 0.56, p < 0.001). Also "Participates in Social Investigation debates" correlates strongly with "Mentioned because of work in Social Investigation" (coefficient = 0.40, p < 0.001). The path coefficients indicate, however, that "Participates in Social Investigation debates" serves to a degree as an intervening factor between senators' preference for social investigation roles and the Ottawa elite's perceptions of actual influence (Prediction [1], path coefficients = 0.10).

The finding that the social investigators who attract the most attention from the Ottawa elite are those who participate in related debates underscores an important aspect of the role as presently acted out in the Senate. Social investigation is largely conducted in special committee studies. These studies involve an immense amount of information gathering; this activity takes up a good part of the total amount of time that the Senate allots for committee work. But after each committee's investigations are over, meetings become less frequent. Many of the members lose interest in its work, but senators who were most active in the investigation turn to the demanding task of preparing the committee's report and presenting it to Parliament and to the public. Hence, participation in Senate debates becomes a crucial vehicle for social investigators who want to keep interest in their favourite cause alive in Parliament.

CONCLUSIONS

This chapter started by discussing "elite accommodation" as one style by which certain sectors of Canadian society influence the federal government. It noted that elite accommodation, as a process, resolves disputes between segments of Canadian society largely through private arrangements between the leaders of various groups. This method diverges from strict polyarchy in that the rank-and-file of groups are often excluded from the decision-making process. The system allows for a fair amount of autonomy among sectors of Canadian society. Yet, as Clement and Presthus point out, this benefit is bought at a high price; among sectors of the economy, business alone gains preferential access to the policy process.

As legislators, then, senators who are business reviewers have benefited the most from this "style", because they often enjoy a high standing in the business community. As well, they exploit to the fullest their institutional resources, especially the Banking, Trade, and Commerce Committee, and are considered influential by the Ottawa political, bureaucratic, and media elite. Recently their work has been rivalled by that of social investigators, who have employed special committees or investigations to influence policy. As a new, non-business elite group, however, social investigators still have not found as permanent and prestigious a vehicle for their work as the business reviewers' Banking Committee. Thus, they have had to speak out from the floor of the Upper House much more frequently, and even travel the country extensively to gain support for their policy proposals.

The chapter which follows adds a pessimistic note to these findings. It shows that recent reforms of the Senate have actually strengthened the hand of business reviewers to the detriment of social investigators. This is especially true of social investigators who depend heavily on their promotional skills to get funds and research assistance for their studies.

NOTES

1. Robert A. Dahl, *Polyarchy: Participation and Opposition* (New Haven, Conn., 1971), pp. 8, 76-80.
2. John Meisel, "Canadian Parties and Politics", in R. H. Leach (ed.), *Contemporary Canada* (Durham, N.C., 1968), p. 135.
3. S. J. R. Noel, "Political Parties and Elite Accommodation: Interpretations of Canadian Federalism", in J. Peter Meekison (ed.), *Canadian Federalism: Myth or Reality* (Toronto, 1971), especially pp. 133-40.
4. Wallace Clement, *The Canadian Corporate Elite: An Analysis of Economic Power* (Toronto, 1975), p. 345.
5. Ibid., p. 349.
6. Robert Presthus, *Elite Accommodation in Canadian Politics* (Toronto, 1973).
7. Robert Presthus, *Elites in the Policy Process* (Toronto, 1974), pp. 146-53.
8. Presthus, *Elite Accommodation*, p. 236.
9. Ibid., p. 226.
10. Ibid., p. 227.
11. The House's Finances, Miscellaneous Estimates, and Public Accounts committees were classified, after factor analysis, as concerned primarily with business review.
12. The best source on uses of factor analysis with dichotomous variables is R. J. Rummel, *Applied Factor Analysis* (Evanston, Ill., 1970), especially p. 217. The analysis employed the program described in Norman H. Nie *et al.*, *Statistical Package for Social Scientists* (New York, 1970), pp. 208-44.
13. The reliability, validity, and invalidity of the additive variable "business review" are an excellent 0.86, 0.93, 0.00, respectively. *Reliability* is a test of a scale based on the assumption that the correlation among items is due to an underlying construct; *validity* assumes that the unique sources of variance among the items were not correlated with other

constructs; *invalidity* refers to the extent to which the scale constructed does not correlate with whatever the items in the scale are measuring. Perfect scores for the respective measures are 1.00, 1.00, and 0. See David R. Heise and George W. Bohrnstedt, "Validity, Invalidity, and Reliability", in Edgar F. Borgatta and George W. Bohrnstedt (eds.), *Sociological Methodology 1970* (San Francisco, 1970), pp. 104-29.

14. Standard deviation is 46; range 0 to 107. The standard deviation is high owing to the relatively large number of respondents who scored 0.
15. Standard deviation is 6.11; range 0 to 37. See note 14.
16. Standard deviation is 5.49; range 0 to 20. See note 14.
17. The average senator received 5.14 nominations from his fellow senators, 3.21 from MPs, 1.24 from civil servants, and 1.69 from members of the parliamentary Press Gallery.
18. Standard deviation is 5.73; range 0 to 45. See note 14.
19. Basic texts on this method are Hubert M. Blalock, Jr., *Causal Inferences in Nonexperimental Research* (Chapel Hill, N.C., 1964); and H. M. Blalock, Jr. (ed.), *Causal Models in Social Sciences* (Chicago, 1971).
20. A measure of the strength of the direct relationship between two variables.
21. A measure which controls intervening influences while ascertaining the affect that one variable in a causal sequence has on subsequent variables.
22. The participation variables are controlled as block constructs. That is, the model controls them: (1) jointly, to examine the over-all intervening importance of participation; and (2) singly, to see if one type of participation has more intervening salience than the other. See John L. Sullivan, "Multiple Indicators and Complex Causal Models", in Blalock (ed.), *Causal Models*, especially pp. 333, 327.
23. Social-cultural committees were Broadcasting, Films, and Assistance to the Arts; Election Expenses; Environment; Health, Welfare, and Social Affairs; Indian Affairs and Northern Development; and Veterans' Affairs; socio-economic resource committees were Agriculture; Fisheries and Forestry; Indian Affairs and Northern Development; Labour, Manpower, and Immigration; National Resources and Public Works; Regional Development; and Transportation and Communication.
24. The reliability, validity, and invalidity of the construct are, respectively, 0.80, 0.88, and 0.03.
25. Standard deviation is 37; range 0 to 123. See note 14.
26. Standard deviation is 7.92; range 0 to 37. See note 14.
27. Standard deviation is 5.11; range 0 to 21. See note 14.
28. Standard deviation is 5.46; range 0 to 48. See note 14.

4.   The Institutional Entrenchment of Business Review

In Chapter 1, we saw that the Senate came under heavy fire in the early 1960s from journalists and politicians. Even John Diefenbaker, the usual defender of existing Canadian institutions, severely denounced the Senate in 1961 for rejecting the Tariffs Bill and giving James Coyne his day in court. At that time, Diefenbaker said apocalyptically:

> the question as to whether or not the Senate of Canada is going beyond that responsibility which it has discharged and can discharge with effectiveness under the constitution is a question the Canadian people will have to decide sooner or later.[1]

Yet Diefenbaker never really acted upon his warning. Almost a year after his prophecy, he introduced to the Commons a relatively tame reform bill which merely required senators to retire at age seventy. The fact that Diefenbaker dissolved Parliament for the federal election of 1962 only ten days after introduction of the Senate reform bill suggests that he was mainly interested in taking a symbolic swipe at the Upper House.[2]

Diefenbaker's bark, that is, was worse than his bite. Nevertheless, the reform movement had gained momentum. The Leader of the Opposition, Lester Pearson, had already beaten Diefenbaker to the draw by urging Senate reform in January 1962. As we saw in Chapter 1, it was Pearson's reform proposal which finally bore fruit. It came in the form of a revised reform bill which Pearson introduced in 1963 when he became Prime Minister. It ultimately won Parliament's approval in 1965. The bill required senators appointed after 1966 to retire at age seventy-five; it also gave other senators the option to retire at age seventy-five with pension. As noted in Chapter 2, the reforms resulted in a mass exodus of older senators from the Upper House and an influx of new blood to fill the vacancies.

Despite these changes, from 1969-71, federal-provincial constitutional conferences mooted radical changes in the Senate's powers, structure, and membership. In response, senators young and old acted vigorously to improve their performances. First, they strengthened standing committees; then they instituted special committees to investigate major social problems; finally they greatly improved their internal resources. Perhaps acting on the belief that it is safer to work with a known quantity than an unknown one, the Pearson and Trudeau governments supported these changes.

This chapter looks at the influx of new blood and senators' concomitant efforts to improve the image of the Upper House. It asks: have such changes affected the *institutional* character of the Senate? It will probe, in addition, to see whether or not the business lobby has consolidated its status as an accepted and established component in the Senate's institutional structure and, therefore, the structure of Parliament as a whole. It will suggest, finally, that social investigation failed to gain a real foothold in the Upper House because business reviewers felt it threatened their monopoly, and thus worked against its ascent.

THE CONCEPT "INSTITUTIONALIZATION"
AS APPLIED TO THE SENATE

Institutionalization is an important dimension of organizational modernization. "Modernization" means adaptation or transformation.[3] An organization modernizes when it enhances its capacity to adjust to "rapid change within its sectors and to events within its total outside environment".

In the past decade, the Canadian Senate has been modernizing to deal with the problems that confront it. Some of these problems flow directly from the fact that Canada is a polyarchy (albeit a modified one) with a Parliament. This state of affairs is by definition a conflict situation.

A polyarchy is a government wherein the politicians often debate political views publicly and the citizens can vote.[4] In a parliamentary form of government, the party with the largest number of seats or the most influence in the lower house of the legislative branch dominates the executive branch. While these two facts seem to complement each other, nevertheless, they disguise two difficulties.

First, in Canada senators are appointed by the Prime Minister; they are not elected. This phenomenon violates one of the canons of polyarchy, which states that legislators should be democratically elected. Thus, senators are usually hand-picked supporters of the Prime Ministers who appointed them. Second, as in many other upper houses in parliamentary systems, the Senate plays only an ancillary role in decision making, and is continually struggling against this limitation.

Institutionalization is a gradual process.[5] An organization, such as the Senate, is on the road to institutionalization when it begins to operate independently and when it establishes a special set of functions which distinguish it from other political organizations.[6] Eventually this organization can accommodate a significant configuration of claimants for benefits and services.[7] In a polyarchy, however, an organization cannot compel members of other organizations to adhere to uniformly centralized patterns of authority. The organization competes in the marketplace for influence, and its ability to do this depends heavily on the extent to which it is institutionalized.

More and more, students of legislatures are beginning to realize that these organizations actually have only a limited impact on political decision making and they are beginning to delineate these limitations for us. Most legislatures, in fact, exercise no *definitive control* over rule making at all in their respective governments.[8] Rather, they perform functions which are auxiliary or even subordinate to rule making. These lesser functions include ratification and promulgation of decisions which have been made elsewhere, information gathering and organization, representation of groups and interests, symbol manipulation (that is, providing the public with cues for responding to legislative actions), administrative control, and adjudication.[9]

Many scholars have maintained that the golden age of legislatures has passed. Some look nostalgically at the nineteenth-century British House of Commons which could make or break governments without recourse to the voters and could control its own timetable.[10] Most attribute this perceived decline of legislatures to the ascendancy of the executive branch in advanced democracies during the twentieth century.[11] Executives, it is said, dominate law making by employing party organizations to mobilize support for key decisions.[12] Presumably, the rapid expansion of mass media has helped executives direct their appeals to broad national constituencies. Such personal appeals can undermine the image of the individual legislator as the representative of the people back home.[13] The legislator's personal power and that of his institution, in other words, become seriously eroded. Bernard Crick reports that as a result of this erosion the British House of Commons, for example, no longer consistently sustains a rule-making function.[14]

Several students of Canada's House of Commons, such as David Hoffman, R. Barry Farrell, C. E. S. Franks, and R. B. Byers, draw conclusions similar to Crick's.[15] They say that the Canadian Commons surveys legislation mainly by criticizing, scrutinizing, and publicizing it.[16] Some scholars do not even grant the Lower House this much power. Paraphrasing Frank H. Underhill, Allan Kornberg says that the House of Commons might well be "a screen behind which the elites who exercise real power are able to operate".[17]

Despite the general decline of power in legislatures, the United States Congress still makes law, although its domain is mainly limited to domestic affairs.[18] Nelson W. Polsby says that a series of "historical accidents" in the late nineteenth century temporarily sent American political parties into disarray, freeing Congress to institutionalize and, thereby, to attain relative autonomy.[19] To a large extent, Congress has operated independently of national parties ever since.

The United States House of Representatives and Senate now employ different strategies for facilitating institutionalization. While the House masters review of the technical details of legislation carried out in specialized committees, the Senate provides a forum from which its members can make statements on public policy issues which have broad national impact.[20] Other legislatures employ similar strategies. In recent years, for example, the British and Canadian legislatures have stressed concern for technical details and have thereby strengthened their committees.[21] The German and French legislatures have also tried to improve the quality and public impact of their policy debates.[22] The Canadian Senate, by emphasizing business review and social investigation, has sought an influence in both the technical and policy development roles. We will find that the institutional changes made by the Senate in recent years have given the edge to the former role. This turn of events occurred despite the fact that the drive toward institutionalization in the late 1960s was supposed to redress imbalances in the Senate's role.

SIGNS OF INSTITUTIONAL MODERNIZATION
IN THE CANADIAN SENATE

The Canadian Senate is not the most heavily institutionalized legislature in the world, but it does enjoy its own distinct identity. One does not simply stroll through the corridors of the Senate wing of Parliament's Centre Block. Visitors have to be checked by security and, unless they have arranged for special status, in order to pass the guards they must prove that they are on their way to visit a particular senator, by appointment. The Senate, thus, is unlike so many of the U.S. state legislatures, where visitors and lobbyists come and go freely, visiting members who have their offices right in the chamber; and where non-members are requested to be seated when votes are taken on the floor.

Walking down a Canadian Senate corridor, the visitor from academe will see offices similar to those of Ivy League college professors who hold endowed chairs. The average senator has a large office with several chairs and a couch, a large desk and bookcase, and numerous political souvenirs and autographed photos—all the symbolic paraphernalia of political efficacy. He or she shares a secretary with one or two other senators. These secretaries usually work in a separate room or in one of the offices of the secretarial pool. The amenities convey one message: senators have worked long in the political vineyard and their labour, or endurance, has paid off.

In the "other house", however, MPS work under opposite conditions. Until recently, most MPS shared their offices with their secretaries. Even with expanded facilities, their quarters mostly resemble those of young scholars who are conducting large research projects while attending to heavy teaching duties and extensive committee obligations. There are so many papers strewn around or piled high and so much hubbub, telephone ringing, and typewriter tapping under pressure of deadlines, that the visiting academic is reminded of a corridor linking the editorial offices of a weekly magazine with national circulation.

Both the Senate and the House of Commons have developed their own styles of operation to fit their particular type of institutionalization. We will examine the Senate's organizational characteristics with reference to three aspects of institutionalization: (1) boundaries—the extent to which the organization is differentiated from its environment; (2) organizational complexity; and (3) universalistic, rather than particularistic, criteria for internal decision making.[23]

Boundaries

In Nelson W. Polsby's terms, "boundary" means identity and exclusivity. Is it difficult to become a member? Do certain individuals share privileges which identify them as members of an organization? Are the organization's leaders recruited from within its own ranks? How then and to what degree has the Senate institutionalized in terms of boundaries?

First, it is difficult to become a senator. As we saw in Chapter 2, many aspire to be senators but few are ultimately chosen for that honour by the Prime Minister. Pierre Elliott Trudeau, for example, was extremely selective when he made his 1968-74 appointments. Like many Prime Ministers before him, despite the availability of nominees with diverse backgrounds he overlooked certain socio-economic sectors and geographic regions of the country in favour of those represented by distinguished party operatives, former public officeholders, and members of the business elite.

Second, with respect to privileges, those who reach the Upper House receive substantial salaries ($24,000) and a tax-free expense allowance ($5,300). Senators also have access to all facilities in Parliament, including the increasingly large research staff of the library. And, finally, senators are permitted generous travel, postal, and telephone privileges which facilitate communication within Canada.

One privilege places senators in an extremely enviable position for legislators: they are appointed to serve until they reach the age of seventy-five. Senators, moreover, have never been asked to depart for partisan reasons.[24] From 1867 to 1965, only 10 per cent of all senators resigned their posts. Of these, the vast majority transferred to other appointive posts, mainly Lieutenant-Governorships or judgeships; several resigned because of ill health or old age; and three departed because of their involvement in political scandals. Maverick traits do have the scope and freedom to flourish in the Senate, as, for example, David Croll's career shows. He has headed up several important special investigations, yet he has been a constant thorn in the side of his party, the Liberals.

Finally, does the Senate actually select its own leaders? The evidence indicates that it usually does not. The length and merit of senatorial careers thus has little effect on the assignment of leadership positions. Both Paul Martin and Ray Perrault, the two most recent Leaders of the Government, virtually parachuted into their posts from the House of Commons. In addition, five current chairmen of Senate standing committees were relative newcomers when they assumed their positions. These are Maurice Lamontagne, Carl Goldenberg, Douglas Everett, Eugene Forsey, and George van Roggen. The partisan nature of a large proportion of Senate appointments, moreover, contributed greatly to the rapid ascent of four of these five senators (Eugene Forsey excepted). It was their record of dedication to the Liberal party, rather than their experience in the Senate *per se* that influenced their colleagues to raise them almost overnight to positions of responsibility in the Upper House. Salter Hayden, of the Banking, Trade, and Commerce Committee, is the longest-tenured committee chairman in the Senate. His status as the "Dean" of chairmen has lent considerable weight to Banking's impact over the years.

Organizational Complexity

"Organizational complexity" refers to the division of labour. Polsby suggests that five phenomena comprise the concept: (1) functions become internally distinct on some regular and explicit basis such as a committee system; (2) parts are no longer wholly interchangeable as members' roles become specialized; (3) the division of labour in the organization parallels its institutionally specified roles; (4) performance expectations are widely shared; (5) there is regularized recruitment to and from roles.[25]

Emile Durkheim said that the division of labour within an organization varies in direct ratio with the volume and density of the society within which it operates.[26] An organization becomes more complex because its society has become regularly denser and generally more voluminous. The growth of governmental expenditures often reflects such growth in the volume and density of society.

The amount that the Canadian government spends has grown rapidly since 1950 (in 1973, it was 557 per cent of the year ending March 1951—see Figure 4.1). While the expenditures of the Senate have grown less rapidly in very recent years than those of the House of Commons, nevertheless they have increased in proportion to the outlays of the federal government (in 1973, they were 552 per cent of the 1951 level). In addition, increases in senators' wages and allowances account for a relatively small portion of this growth. Senators' salaries currently are 387 per cent of the 1951 level; permanent staffs' wages and other operating expenses have attained 446 and

Figure 4.1 The rate of increase of Senate expenditures, although slower than that of the House of Commons, has kept abreast of the growth of federal government spending (percentages based on 1951 figures)

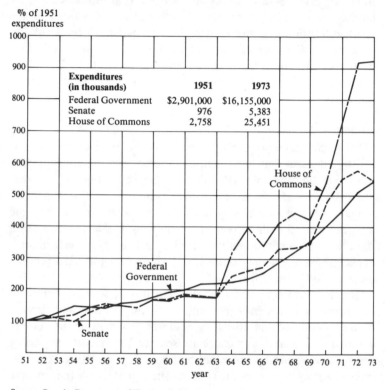

% of 1951
expenditures

Expenditures (in thousands)	1951	1973
Federal Government	$2,901,000	$16,155,000
Senate	976	5,383
House of Commons	2,758	25,451

Source: Canada, Department of Finance, *Public Accounts*, 1951-73.

3625 per cent of the 1951 level, respectively. Thus, individual senators have vastly greater resources to call upon as they perform their legislative tasks than they did in 1951.

As we see in Figure 4.1, the degree to which Senate expenditures have kept up with growth in the federal government and the House of Commons outlays has varied according to governments. During the St. Laurent government (Liberals, 1948-57), the expenditure growth rates trailed slightly behind those of the federal government and the House of Commons. None of the rates of increase, however, was dramatic. While John Diefenbaker was Prime Minister (Progressive Conservative, 1957-63), Senate expenditures grew at a slightly higher rate than those of the House of Commons. Still, growth occurred only very gradually. When Lester Pearson (Liberal, 1963-68) took office as Prime Minister, the growth rate of House of Commons' spending shot far beyond that of the federal government and the Senate. Senate spending during this period, however, attained a higher level in proportion to its 1951 figure than did that of the federal government. Pierre Elliott Trudeau's government (Liberal, 1968-present) ushered in the highest rate of expenditure growth for the federal government, the Senate, and the House of Commons. The House of Commons came out, by a large margin, as the principal beneficiary of this trend. The Senate expenditures maintained a higher level relative to 1951 than those of the federal government until 1973. In that year, Senate spending took a sharp dip. No doubt this was due in part to the fact that Trudeau came through the 1972 election with a minority government which depended on the support of the anti-Senate New Democratic party and lasted until 1974.

The fact that Senate expenditures have risen in proportion to federal government spending suggests that the level of organizational complexity, especially the division of labour in the Upper House, has increased considerably since 1951. The degree to which increased spending resulted mainly from operations' costs lends further credence to this expectation.

The distribution of Senate work has changed drastically since 1953 in sittings of the entire House and meetings of standing and special committees. The changes largely substantiate the expectation that the Senate, in addition to claiming a share of resources proportionate to increases in federal government expenditures, has tried to cope with growth in government by employing the division of labour. The number of Senate sittings per session day has declined quite significantly, especially since 1963 (see Table 4.1). This decline might have been the result partially of the fact that the Liberal party regained control of the House of Commons in 1963, and so no longer felt compelled to play the loyal opposition in the Senate. A corresponding decline in the sittings per session day, however, has occurred in the House of Commons. Much of this falling off in numbers of parliamentary sittings might be explained by increased use of committees in both the House and Senate. Table 4.1 indicates, in fact, that Senate committee activity offsets the relative infrequency of sittings.

Committees of the Canadian Senate reveal remarkable activity and productivity when compared to committees in political systems other than the United States. Specialist committees in the British House of Commons, for example, have been plagued by a curious series of frustrations. John P. Mackintosh tells us that these difficulties include severe limitations on travel, particularly to foreign countries, late and incomplete testimony from Cabinet Ministers, and infrequent debate of committee reports in the House.[27] Committees in the Canadian Parliament, on the other hand, have increased their ability not only to conduct studies but also, in some instances, to survey government legislation. This trend has developed most rapidly since 1968 when parliamentary committees received a mandate from the Trudeau government to modernize and to professionalize.

Senate standing committees have thus been strengthened. As a result, their review of specific bills has gained influence, as have their special investigations in anticipation of policy changes. To assure that committees operate more efficiently, Senate rules have required, since 1969, that the Internal Economy Committee approve budgets for specific investigations and, since 1973, that committee membership be held to twenty-two senators.

The Banking, Trade, and Commerce, and National Finance committees are the most active standing committees. Since 1953 they have accounted for more than half of the standing committee meetings (Table 4.1). The Banking Committee, in addition, uses the largest share of the funds granted to standing committees (Table 4.2).

During the late 1960s and early 1970s, enterprising social investigators such as Senators David Croll, Keith Davey, and

Table 4.1 THE SITTINGS PER SESSION DAY OF THE SENATE HAVE DECLINED IN RECENT YEARS WHILE COMMITTEE ACTIVITY HAS INCREASED GREATLY

| Parliament | Session Days | Senate | | | | | House of Commons |
		Meetings/ Session Day of Senate B, T & C Finance	Meetings/ Session Day of Senate All Standing Committees	Meetings/ Session Day of Senate Special & Joint Committees	Total of Meetings/ Session Day All Committees	Sittings of Senate/ Session Day	Sittings/ Session Day
(22) 1953-57	787	.03	.05	.12	.17	.36	.54
(23) 1957-58	111	.02	.05	.027	.072	.40	.70
(24) 1958-62	919	.10	.14	.11	.25	.38	.66
(25) 1962-63	132	.09	.10	.015	.11	.32	.54
(26) 1963-65	788	.10	.15	.058	.20	.26	.53
(27) 1965-68	828	.14	.21	.31	.52	.22	.49
(28) 1968-72	1253	.18	.31	.34	.65	.25	.47

Compiled by author

Table 4.2 EXPENDITURES OF SENATE COMMITTEES SINCE 1968
(in Thousands of Dollars)

Committee	Question	Duration of Study	Funds Spent for Study	Total Funds Spent Since 1968
Agriculture	General	1st sess., 29th Parl.	27	64
	,,	1st sess., 30th Parl.	37	
Banking, Trade, and Commerce	Tax reform	1969-73	444	696
	Budget resolutions related to income tax	1st sess., 29th Parl.	8	
	Foreign investment	1st sess., 29th Parl.	42	
	General	1st sess., 30th Parl.	202	
Employer-Employee Relations (Joint)		1st sess., 30th Parl.	50	50
Foreign Affairs	Caribbean area	1970-71	75	254
	Pacific	1970-73	91	
	Europe	1972-74	38	
	U. S.	2nd sess., 29th Parl.	13	
	U. S.	1st sess., 30th Parl.	37	
Legal and Constitutional Affairs	Parole system in Canada	1971-74	183	200
	,,	2nd sess., 29th Parl.	16	
	Cannabis	1st sess., 30th Parl.	1	
Mass Media (Special)	—	1969-71	621	621
National Finance	Potential growth	1971-72	128	248
	General	1st sess., 29th Parl.	26	
	,,	1st sess., 30th Parl.	94	
Poverty (Special)	—	1969-73	769	769
Regulations and other Statutory Instruments (Joint)	General	2nd sess., 29th Parl.	22	105
	,,	1st sess., 30th Parl.	83	
Science Policy (Special)	—	1968-73	701	856
		1st sess., 30th Parl.	155	
		Grand sum		3,863

SOURCE: Administration and Personnel Branch, The Senate, and *Minutes of the Proceedings of the Senate* (1974-76).

Maurice Lamontagne engaged in vigorous and expensive studies of the social ills of the country. As a result, they rivalled Banking's and National Finance's use of funds assigned to committees. Indeed, during 1969-73, the Poverty, Mass Media, and Science Policy committees each spent more than the combined $572,000 spent by Banking and National Finance.

The mid-seventies have seen a sharp decline in social investigators' claims on Senate resources. Only Lamontagne's Science Policy Committee has survived the "taming" of social investigators—in which their studies have either been discontinued or subsumed by standing committees, particularly by the Legal and Constitutional Affairs Committee (see Chapter 1). The Legal Committee, in fact, spent only $1,000 in the first session of the thirtieth Parliament while Banking and National Finance spent $296,000. Although the Standing Committee on Foreign Affairs has drawn large sums through the mid-seventies, its work, which centres mainly on special studies of economic relations between Canada and various other countries, falls more within the ambit of business review than social investigation. Senate committee expenditures since 1968 indicate, then, that, despite the spurt of success for some enterprising social investigators from 1968 to 1973, business reviewers actually consolidated their dominance of Senate resources by the mid-seventies.

Universalistic Criteria

Polsby tells us that a highly institutionalized legislature makes internal decisions (e.g., assignment of committee chairmanships) based on universalistic rather than on particularistic criteria.[28] By "universalistic criteria" he means those methods, such as precedents and impersonal codes, which are applied consistently on the basis of seniority or even of merit. These criteria replace discretionary methods for conducting internal business. According to discretionary methods, favouritism and nepotism strongly influence the assignment of tasks and resources; partisan interests, in other words, dominate.

The Senate has rules and orders which are codified, and the application of these is the duty of the Speaker. Senators devote a fair amount of time to the discussion of these codes. Since 1970, the Senate also has kept a careful eye on its budget.[29] When the Senate gives a committee the go-ahead on an investigation, that committee must now submit its budget to the Internal Economy Committee for approval. The committee must also publish its budget and eventual expenditures in the *Minutes of the Proceedings of the Senate.* One clear index of this new budgetary concern is the fact that the Internal Economy Committee, which used to meet only once or twice a session, met nine times in a recent session (1973-74).

No parliamentary committee, whether Senate, House of Commons, or Joint, may enlist staff beyond the duration of current sessions. The allocation of staff to Senate committees, thus, often reflects the whim of the Internal Economy Committee which, in turn, frequently defers to the priorities of the Leader of the Government in the Senate. In April 1975, however, Senator Eugene Forsey appealed this procedure. As chairman of the Joint Committee on Regulations and other Statutory Instruments, he appealed to the public forum and threatened to resign if he could not engage a long-term legal and secretarial staff. Forsey got what he wanted. It is still too soon, however, to determine whether he set a precedent.

The assignment of investigations to various committees represents a point of contention for members who expect even-handed treatment. Essentially, the Government Leader decides what work goes to what committees. He holds his office from the Prime Minister; and his staff, which divides its time fairly equally between Cabinet, Senate, and provincial affairs (in the case of Perrault, B.C.), is financed entirely by the $130,000 granted to Cabinet Ministers for the operation of their parliamentary offices. The Leader then knows well what the Cabinet wants and how to implement its interests. He sometimes snaps proposed studies right out of the hands of such maverick senators as David Croll, Chesley Carter, or Hazen Argue, and gives them to committee chairmen whom he considers "dependable"; these include Salter Hayden or Carl Goldenberg (Legal and Constitutional Affairs). As a result, a backlog of studies piles up on the agendas of favoured committees.

In one aspect of committee life, however, the Leader has little direct involvement: it is in the assignment of committee positions. Rather, the Committee of Selection performs this task. The party whips shoulder most of the responsibility for sorting through senators' requests for assignments and coming to amicable agreements. The competition for some committee positions is extremely stiff. Many senators, for instance, work diligently on the less influential National Finance Committee merely to attract the attention of important Banking members who might support their bids for spots on the latter committee. We might expect thus that such influential committees as Banking or Internal Economy would have older members and relatively few vacancies from session to session. Presumably, once a senator has attained an enviable position he will be loath to relinquish it.

The average ages and turnover of committee members for each session from 1966 to 1975 disputes this hypothesis. Three housekeeping committees (Library, Printing, and Restaurant) have the oldest senators and a fairly low turnover in membership. The Banking Committee, during the period in question, had almost a median average age (sixty-six) and the second-highest turnover. Most committees with low average ages for membership have fairly low turnover. The findings then suggest the operation of a merit system in committee assignments rather than a seniority system whereby preference is given to age. Very old senators tend to end up in housekeeping committees where they remain until they leave the Senate. Other committees are purged of inactive senators from time to time. This was true of Standing Orders in 1968 (twenty-eighth Parliament, first session), when Hartland Molson spearheaded the reform of Senate rules; and of Internal Economy in 1969 (twenty-eighth Parliament, second session), when the budgetary process of the Senate was tightened. The most dramatic turnover, however, occurred in Banking where the new members joining the committee in four different parliamentary sessions (28: 1, 3, 4; 29: 1) amounted to 30 per cent. This finding points up the degree to which many are called but few are chosen on Salter Hayden's prestigious committee. That is, if a member of the Banking Committee does not fulfil the expectations of Hayden and other key members, there are plenty of aspirants who can take his place. Relatively low proportions of vacancies on some of the less influential committees which focus on legislative fields (e.g., Health, Welfare, and Science; and Agriculture) suggest that senators do not compete intensely for these positions. The Committee of Selection, thus, must have to place particular emphasis on matters besides merit in making assignments. If competition for positions on a committee is low, this limits Selection's pool of recruits. The Selection Committee, in these instances, is likely to stick with regular members who fulfil other criteria, such as partisan and regional representation.

CONCLUSIONS

In this chapter we have seen how the Senate is modernizing. That is, in recent years it has adjusted its institutional structure so as to perform its two principal roles with more efficiency and impact. The two roles, of course, are business review and social investigation. Of the two, the former has benefited the most from institutionalization.

With respect to boundaries, senators have at their disposal many of the amenities and privileges of MPs; new appointees emerge from a competitive nomination process which is nevertheless controlled mainly by the Prime Minister and the Cabinet; and leaders within the Upper House mainly owe their positions either to the Prime Minister or to the Senate's Government Leader. The Senate then is well-bounded with respect to amenities and privileges, and to the difficulty of obtaining appointments; it is poorly bounded in that senators owe both their seats and leadership positions within the Senate to the executive branch. Two characteristics of Senate appointment, however, mitigate Senate dependence on the executive. First, the fact that senators are appointed until age seventy-five allows some maverick senators to act independently of the executive branch. Second, the bias in the appointment system which favours Liberal party operatives, former public office-holders, and members of the business elite provides a core group of senators who possess all three traits. Such senators have considerable personal resources, political and socio-economic, which, when pooled, add immense substance and resilience to the lobby from within.

Organizational complexity within the Senate has increased considerably in proportion to the federal government's expenditures. The rapid rate at which committee meetings have replaced sittings of the Senate as the principal forums for legislative work indicates the degree to which division of labour has taken hold in the Upper House. The intensified activity of the business-review oriented Banking and National Finance committees accounts for a very large portion of this division of labour, both in terms of standing committee meetings and funds expended. On the other hand, the recent channelling of social investigatory work through standing (mainly Legal and Constitutional Affairs) rather than special committees has sharply reduced the amounts available for this type of legislative work.

With respect to internal decision making, impartiality has replaced favouritism to only a limited degree. Senators now spend a fairly large amount of time discussing procedural matters; they also review their operational budget very closely. But the Government Leader still shows favouritism when he assigns investigations to committees. The Banking, Trade, and Commerce, and, recently, the Legal and Constitutional Affairs committees have benefited the most from this favouritism. As indicated by the very high turnover in its membership, Banking, in addition, has experienced several purges of personnel. This finding probably reflects the firm guidance of Salter Hayden who has been tolerant neither of unproductive nor of uncooperative senators.

In sum, the Senate has institutionalized greatly, especially in the last decade. When the retirement reform went into effect in 1965, new members infused new lifeblood into the Upper House; likewise when the constitutional conferences challenged the Senate's performance (1968-71), young and old senators alike worked to improve their institution. As a result, special committees to investigate social problems began to flourish. At first it seemed that the revitalized and modernized Senate would achieve a new and more equitable balance between business review and social investigation. By the mid-1970s, however, business reviewers had taken back much of the committee resources and powers from the reform-minded social investigators (that is, they absorbed many of the younger senators into their committees and drew off much of the financial and time allotments for committee work).

Chapter 5 will argue that it is the appointive process which ultimately turned the reform impulse toward a strengthening of the lobby from within. Young or old, freshly appointed or emeritus, innovative or hidebound, senators maintain an Upper House where the business lobby prevails because they owe their seats mostly to partisan, political, and business connections.

NOTES

1. Henry S. Albinski, "The Canadian Senate: Politics and the Constitution", *American Political Science Review*, 57 (1963), p. 384. Albinski quotes Diefenbaker from *House of Commons Debates*, July 6, 1961, p. 7626.
2. Ibid., pp. 388-89.
3. Allan Kornberg, Samuel M. Hines, Jr., and Joel Smith, "Legislatures and the Modernization of Societies", *Comparative Political Studies*, 5 (January 1973), p. 475.
4. Robert A. Dahl, *Polyarchy: Participation and Opposition* (New Haven, Conn., 1971), p. 4.
5. Richard Sisson, "Comparative Legislative Institutionalization: A Theoretical Explanation", in Allan Kornberg (ed.), *Legislatures in Comparative Perspective* (New York, 1973), p. 19.
6. Samuel P. Huntington, *Political Order in Changing Societies* (New Haven, Conn., 1968), pp. 20-22.
7. Sisson, "Comparative Legislative Institutionalization", p. 19.
8. John C. Wahlke *et al.*, *The Legislative System* (New York, 1962), p. 6; and Edward W. Muller, "The Representation of Citizens by Political Authorities: Consequences for Regime Support", *American Political Science Review*, 64 (December 1970), p. 1151.
9. Wahlke, *The Legislative System*, p. 6.
10. John P. Mackintosh, "Reform of the House of Commons: The Case for Specialization", in Gerhard Loewenberg (ed.), *Modern Parliaments: Change or Decline?* (Chicago, 1971), p. 35; and Peter Gerlich, "The Institutionalization of European

Parliaments", in Kornberg, *Legislatures in Comparative Perspective*, p. 98.

11. François Goguel, "Parliament under the Fifth French Republic: Difficulties of Adapting to a New Role", in Loewenberg, *Modern Parliaments*, p. 93; and Philip Williams, "Parliament under the Fifth French Republic: Patterns of Executive Domination", in Loewenberg, *Modern Parliaments*, p. 101.

12. Malcolm E. Jewell, "Linkages Between Legislative Parties and External Parties", in Kornberg, *Legislatures in Comparative Perspective*, pp. 205-11.

13. Nelson W. Polsby, "Strengthening Congress in National Policymaking", in Nelson W. Polsby (ed.), *Congressional Behavior* (New York, 1971), p. 5.

14. Bernard Crick, "Parliament in the British Political System", in Allan Kornberg and Lloyd D. Musolf (eds.), *Legislatures in Developmental Perspective* (Durham, N.C., 1970), pp. 33-54.

15. David Hoffman, "Liaison Officers and Ombudsmen: Canadian MPs and Their Relations with the Federal Bureaucracy and Executive", in Thomas A. Hockin (ed.), *Apex of Power* (Toronto, 1971), p. 150; R. Barry Farrell, *The Making of Canadian Foreign Policy* (Toronto, 1969), p. 144; C. E. S. Franks, "The Dilemma of the Standing Committees of the Canadian House of Commons", *Canadian Journal of Political Science*, 4 (December 1971), pp. 461-76; and R. B. Byers, "Perceptions of Parliamentary Surveillance of the Executive: The Case of Canadian Defence Policy", *Canadian Journal of Political Science*, 5 (June 1972), pp. 234-50.

16. Byers, "Perceptions of Parliamentary Surveillance", p. 235.

17. Allan Kornberg and Lloyd D. Musolf, "On Legislatures in Developmental Perspective", in Kornberg and Musolf, *Legislatures in Developmental Perspective*, p. 15.

18. Roger H. Davidson, "Congress in the American Political System", in Kornberg and Musolf, *Legislatures in Developmental Perspective*, pp. 134-42.

19. Polsby, "Strengthening Congress in National Policymaking", p. 5.

20. Ibid., pp. 6-7.

21. Mackintosh, "Reform of the House of Commons", pp. 33-65; Byers, "Perceptions of Parliamentary Surveillance", pp. 234-350; Franks, "Dilemma of the Standing Committees".

22. Wilhelm Hennis, "Reform of the Bundestag: The Case for General Debate", in Locwenberg, *Modern Parliaments*, pp. 65-79; Goguel, "Parliament under the Fifth French Republic: Difficulties", pp. 81-95; Williams, "Parliament under the Fifth French Republic: Executive Domination", pp. 97-109.

23. Nelson W. Polsby, "The Institutionalization of the U.S. House

of Representatives", *American Political Science Review*, 62 (March 1968), p. 145.

24. See W. F. Dawson, "Resignation and Removal of Canadian Senators", *The Parliamentarian*, 56 (January 1975), pp. 12-20.
25. Polsby, "Institutionalization", pp. 153-58, 164.
26. Emile Durkheim, *The Division of Labor in Society*, translated by George Simpson (New York, 1964), p. 262.
27. Mackintosh, "Reform of the House of Commons", pp. 41-52.
28. Polsby, "Institutionalization", pp. 160-64.
29. *Debates of the Senate* (October 22, 1970), pp. 41-42.

5. Influences on Senators' Choice of Roles: Sources of the Dominance of Business Review

In the previous chapter we learned that the Senate has become a more complex and efficient institution in the last decade. We learned also that business reviewers have reaped the benefits of this change. Social investigators, on the other hand, have lost the power and the prestige they were on the verge of wresting from business reviewers in the late sixties and early seventies. Today they are slipping into the background of Senate life. Why has social investigation failed to become a permanent, influential part of legislative activity in the Upper House? This chapter asserts that senators who choose business review as their role do so in response to a clearer and more powerful set of influences than do social investigators. When linked to the appointment process of the Senate, these influences explain why and how business reviewers became the dominant block in the Senate.

This dominant block I call the lobby from within. In Chapter 2 we saw how the appointive process often assures Canada of senators who will easily adapt to the role of lobbying for the business community. That is, the process produces senators who: (1) with respect to political environment, come disproportionately from the urban centres of their provinces, most notably from the nation's two business and financial centres, Toronto and Montreal; (2) with respect to socio-economic and political background, frequently come from the cream of both the business and political communities; (3) with respect to behavioural orientations, most often view themselves as particularly qualified to bring the business-legal viewpoint to legislative review; (4) with respect to institutional orientations, tend to view themselves as statesmen who limit their communication with those outside the Senate and represent the country as a whole by transcending particularistic claims from provinces or regions.

This chapter hypothesizes that political environments from which many senators come, their socio-economic and political backgrounds, their behavioural orientations, and their institutional orientations combine to produce extremely intense aptitudes and desires among many senators for bringing the marketplace ethic to their legislative work. The intensity of this ethic in the Senate translates into a clear dominance of business reviewers over social investigators in the struggle to decide which type of emphasis will be placed on legislative review. As opposed to social investigators, business reviewers have institutional orientations reinforced by behavioural orientations. Their behavioural orientations, in turn, are supported by their socio-economic and political backgrounds. Their socio-economic and political backgrounds, specifically their links with the nation's business and political elite, are strengthened by the types of political environments from which they come. The various factors which influence social investigators to choose their legislative role, on the other hand, relate to each other much less coherently. This chapter tests these expectations, first presenting a picture of exactly which political environment, socio-economic, behavioural, and institutional orientation factors most strongly influence senators to choose either business review or social investigation.

KEY INFLUENCES ON
SENATORS' LEGISLATIVE ROLE PERCEPTIONS

Chapter 2's profile of senators' traits was developed from four distinct conceptual domains which might help predict what kinds of senators become business reviewers or social investigators. These areas were: political environment, socio-economic and political background, behavioural orientations, and institutional orientations. This present section considers each of these domains in order to discover which traits most affect senators' views of the two legislative roles. What we learned about business reviewers and social investigators in Chapters 2 and 3 suggests several hypotheses about the main influences on senators' choice of the roles. Because of the conservative bent of their role, we might expect the following to be, by and large, true of business reviewers.

(1) They come from urban areas and from provinces which are well represented in the Upper House and where there is fairly strong support for the Progressive Conservative or Social Credit parties and relatively little political competition.

(2) They are older senators, long-term residents of Ontario or Quebec, and those who belong to the socio-economic upper crust in that they are lawyers, businessmen, Protestants, Anglo-Saxons, and well educated; senators who are Progressive Conservatives, have leadership positions in their parliamentary party of the Senate, have long tenure in the Upper House, or are relatively experienced in public office or extra-parliamentary party leadership.

(3) They are also senators who got into politics for partisan reasons, because someone in their youth inspired them, or because they wanted to exercise their occupational expertise; and senators who report that they are only part-time legislators.

(4) They feel accountable to their party, consult party sources for advice on bills, and communicate infrequently with "constituents".

Social investigators, on the other hand, are reformers; as such, we might hypothesize that they will mostly be:

(1) Senators from heavily urban areas and provinces which are underrepresented in the Senate, and where, although political competition is relatively high, there is strongest support for the Liberal and NDP parties;

(2) Younger, short-tenured Liberal senators from Ontario and Quebec who do not belong to the socio-economic upper crust, do not hold leadership positions in the Senate, and are relatively inexperienced in public and party offices outside of the Senate.

(3) Senators who say that they got into politics and Parliament for altruistic reasons and call themselves "full-time legislators".

(4) Senators who believe that they are especially responsive to extra-parliamentary structures and report a great deal of communication with their "constituents".

These hypotheses do not specify which influences within the four sets of independent variables on the two legislative role scales are the strongest. The available literature in this field is simply too limited. The analysis, therefore, employs stepwise multiple regression to ascertain the relative strength of the linkages between the independent variables and the two role types.[1] Tables 5.1 and 5.2 report the findings of these regressions. The tables list only those results which approach statistical significance at at least the 0.05 level.

Business Review

The variable "business review" was regressed first on the eleven "constituency" political environment items (see Table 5.1). Only one relation was strong enough, statistically, to warrant comment. Senators from heavily urban areas show the strongest preference for the role. This finding makes sense. Because most of Canada's business is done in very large cities, senators from these centres often bring the business view of things to bear on legislation. This observation finds support in the only notable result of the regression of "business review" on the provincial-political-environment variables. Senators from those provinces with the most MPs, namely Ontario and Quebec, more often choose business review as their role. Ontario and Quebec have Canada's two major financial and commercial centres, Toronto and Montreal.

With respect to social background, the study predicted that lawyers in the Senate would disproportionately choose business review. Presumably, legal training equips senators for the arduous clause-by-clause review of bills which the role involves. This prediction finds support in the analysis. The data, however, indicate that senators who have served as directors of corporations become business reviewers far more often than lawyers do.

Table 5.1 "BUSINESS REVIEW" REGRESSED ON . . .

Variables	Correlation Coefficient (Simple r)	Normalized Regression Coefficient (Beta Score)	Multiple Regression Coefficient (r Square)
1. Political Environment			
a. "Constituency"			
i) % of population urban	.23	.23	.05
ii) % of vote Social Credit	.12	.14	.07
iii) Near perfect competition between parties in area	−.13	−.13	.09
b. Province			
i) # of House of Commons seats	.18	.18	.03
2. Background Characteristics			
a. Social			
i) # of *firms* for which senator is a director	.51[a]	.51[a]	.26[a]
ii) Roman Catholic	−.16	−.18	.29[a]
iii) Lawyer	.29[b]	.15	.31[a]
iv) Businessman	.08	.19	.34[a]
b. Political			
i) Progressive Conservative	.20	.20	.04
ii) Has held *provincial* public office	−.13	−.19	.10
iii) Has held *local* public office	.14	.19	.13
3. Behavioural Orientations			
i) Senator attributed selection of favourite committee to occupation	.40[a]	.40[a]	.16[a]
ii) Got into politics for partisan reasons	.27[b]	.24[b]	.22[a]
iii) Senator attributes speciality to occupational expertise	.33[a]	.17	.25[a]
iv) Main occupation is being a senator	.13	−.26	.28[a]
4. Institutional Orientations			
i) Feels accountable to party	.63[a]	.63[a]	.39[a]
ii) Constituents communicate by phone and personal visit	−.16	−.23[b]	.45[a]
iii) Uses structured extra-party sources for information on bills	−.20	−.13	.46[a]
iv) Is expansive in the type of sources he/she consults	−.01	−.14	.48[a]

[a]significant at 0.01 level   [b]significant at 0.05 level

The regression of business review on the socio-economic variables also suggests that Roman Catholics choose the role less frequently than other senators. The finding supports Porter's claim that some religious and ethnic backgrounds limit the types of roles certain elites can or will choose.

The analysis regressed the "business review" scale on seventeen political background variables. Table 5.1 shows the results. They suggest only one relation, and minimally at that; that is, that Progressive Conservatives often actively select business review. Yet even this relation falls short of statistical significance. Although the hypothesis stated that senators with political experience would prefer business review, the findings indicate that this is not so; indeed senators with no previous provincial offices prefer business review to a limited degree. Peculiarities of business review might explain these findings. The role, obviously, calls upon talents other than political acumen alone. A lack of business knowledge and contacts probably precludes the possibility of many politically experienced senators becoming business reviewers.

The regression of "business review" on the behavioural orientations corresponds clearly to the hypotheses. Senators who say that they chose their specialities and committee work because they wanted to use their occupational expertise and those who say they entered politics for partisan reasons strongly favour the role. Senators who consider themselves part-time legislators likewise favour the role. Business reviewers, then, do not seem to be motivated by their political careers *per se*. Many of them got into politics through partisan loyalty; now that they are in the Senate they want mainly to lend the business viewpoint to legislative review.

Finally, business reviewers overwhelmingly hold themselves accountable to their parties and report relatively few calls and visits from constituents. This result is just as the study predicted. In addition there is evidence that they avoid consulting extra-party organizations about bills.

Social Investigation
The regression of "social investigation" on the "constituency" political environment variables produced one expected relation

(see Table 5.2). Senators from competitive areas do prefer social investigation although not overwhelmingly. It is paradoxical, considering the social-reform bent of the NDP and the free-enterprise orientation of Social Credit, that senators from areas with a strong NDP vote avoid the role, while those from areas which are heavily Social Credit actively seek the role.

Clearly, senators who come from provinces with certain types of political environments chose social investigation. These were provinces which are overrepresented in the Upper House because of their relatively small population, those in which a senator's party is in a favourable competitive position in terms of House-of-Commons seats, and those in which party competition, in terms of votes, is low. These findings indicate that the predictions were wrong. The somewhat economically depressed Atlantic provinces, however, are the ones which are overrepresented in the Senate; and they do have many non-competitive federal constituencies. A phenomenon might exist of course whereby Atlantic-provinces senators are concerned with social reform even if they are not from heavily urban areas, and even if much of the electoral environment does not strongly reinforce the orientation.

With respect to the regression of "social investigation" on the social background variables, the data indeed show that senators who were born and raised in, and represent the Atlantic provinces do overwhelmingly choose social investigation. Social investigators, in addition, tend to be French Canadians, to have received some of their education outside their own province, and not to be lawyers and/or businessmen. With the exception of education, then, these traits support the hypothesis that social investigators would have relatively humble socio-economic backgrounds.

As was the case with "business review", the regression of "social investigation" on the political background variables provides relatively weak and ambiguous results. There is some slight indication that senators with experience in public office, especially in federal positions, prefer social investigation. This finding runs counter to our hypotheses. Yet, in line with these expectations, experience in federal party offices seems to reduce the likelihood that senators will adopt the role. These results argue that only very cautious assertions should be made about the influence political background has on senators' choice of social investigation.

Table 5.2   "SOCIAL INVESTIGATION" REGRESSED ON . . .

Variables	Correlation Coefficient (Simple r)	Normalized Regression Coefficient (Beta Score)	Multiple Regression Coefficient (r Square)
1. Political Environment			
a. "Constituency"			
i) Difference between votes won by the strongest and second strongest parties is great	−.17	−.17	.03
ii) % of vote NDP	−.15	−.16	.06
iii) % of vote Social Credit	.16	.14	.08
b. Province			
i) Ratio of % of Senate seats held by province over % of House of Commons seats	.30[b]	.30[b]	.09[b]
ii) Senator's party is in a favourable competitive position in province in terms of seats in House of Commons	.20	.25[b]	.15[a]
iii) Near perfect competition in % of vote received by all parties in province	.26[b]	−.17	.17[a]
2. Background			
a. Social			
i) Born, raised in, and represents Atlantic provinces	.38[a]	.38[a]	.14[a]
ii) Educated out of province	.21	.21	.19[a]
iii) French	.08	.23[b]	.24[a]
iv) Age	−.02	−.17	.26[a]
iv) Lawyer	−.26[b]	−.14	.28[a]
vi) Businessman	−.08	−.24[b]	.32[a]
vii) Educational attainment	.07	.28	.35[a]
b. Political			
i) Has held party office on *federal* level	−.19	−.19	.04
ii) Has held public office on *federal* level	.17	.16	.06
iii) # of levels on which party offices held	−.06	.22	.09

Variables	Correlation Coefficient (Simple r)	Normalized Regression Coefficient (Beta Score)	Multiple Regression Coefficient (r Square)
3. Behavioural Orientations			
i) Senator attributes selection of favourite committee to civic-altruistic motives	.45[a]	.45[a]	.20[a]
ii) Senator's suggestions for revisions derive from occupational expertise	.34[a]	.25[b]	.26[a]
iii) Senator attributes speciality to civic-altruistic motives	.23	.22[b]	.31[a]
iv) Senator's suggestions for revisions derive from civic-altruistic motives	.14	.14	.33[a]
4. Institutional Orientations			
i) Uses structured extra-party sources for information on bills	.26[b]	.26[b]	.07[b]
ii) Constituents communicate by phone and personal visit	.21	.19	.10[b]
iii) Feels accountable to extra-party institutions	.18	.17	.13[b]
iv) Legislative focus is on local policy issues	.17	.15	.15[b]

[a]significant at 0.01 level   [b]significant at 0.05 level

The findings on the behavioural orientations partially support the predictions. Senators who chose their specialities and their favourite committees because of altruistic impulses clearly prefer social investigation. But senators who chose their specialities because they wanted to exercise some occupational expertise in the area of legislative revision equally prefer social investigation.

The relationship between senators' institutional orientations and their choice of "social investigation" supports some of the predictions. To a significant degree, social investigators do consult extra-party structures for advice on bills and they do often hold themselves accountable to these "outsiders". Furthermore, there is evidence that constituents frequently talk to these senators by phone or in person.

Figure 5.1 The Interrelatedness of Influences on Business Review

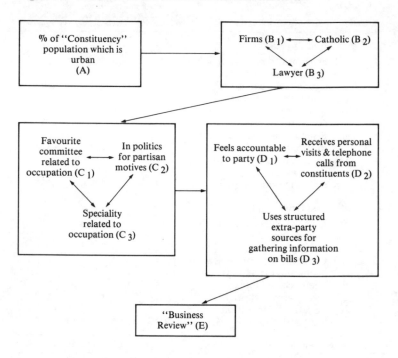

CAUSAL ANALYSES

The Interrelatedness of Influences on "Business Review"

Figure 5.1 outlines the first causal analysis. The model portrays the way in which we might expect the four categories of variables to interrelate as influences on senators' choice of business review as a legislative role. These categories are: political environment ("constituency"), social background, behavioural orientations, and institutional orientations. Let us briefly review here what we have learned about senators who prefer business review:

A. They mainly reside in urban federal constituencies.

B. They usually have elite social backgrounds; many are non-Catholic lawyers who hold a number of directorships in business firms.

c. They tend to believe that their committee work and specialities flow naturally from their occupation, and they are likely to be in politics for partisan reasons.

Table 5.3 ASSUMPTIONS ABOUT THE INTERRELATEDNESS OF INFLUENCES ON "BUSINESS REVIEW"

Assumption	Pearson's Correlation Coefficient	Expected/ Actual Direction of Relation
1. $rAB \neq 0$		
(1) rab_1	= .14	+/+
(2) rab_2	= $.24^a$	−/+
(3) rab_3	= $.27^b$	+/+
2. $rBC \neq 0$		
(1) rb_1c_1	= $.27^b$	+/+
(2) rb_2c_1	= $-.20^b$	−/−
(3) rb_3c_1	= .19	+/+
(4) rb_1c_2	= $.25^b$	+/+
(5) rb_2c_2	= .01	−/+
(6) rb_3c_2	= .06	+/+
(7) rb_1c_3	= $.29^a$	+/+
(8) rb_2c_3	= −.04	−/−
(9) rb_3c_3	= .09	+/+
3. $rCD \neq 0$		
(1) rc_1d_1	= $.42^a$	+/+
(2) rc_2d_1	= $.28^a$	+/+
(3) rc_3d_1	= .14	+/+
(4) rc_1d_2	= −.02	−/−
(5) rc_2d_2	= .07	−/+
(6) rc_3d_2	= −.14	−/−
(7) rc_1d_3	= −.05	−/−
(8) rc_2d_3	= .07	−/+
(9) rc_3d_3	= .01	−/+
4. $rDE \neq 0$		
(1) rd_1e	= $.63^a$	+/+
(2) rd_2e	= −.16	−/−
(3) rd_3e	= −.20	−/−

[a]significant at 0.01 level   [b]significant at 0.05 level

D. They usually feel accountable to their party above all; many say that they rarely communicate with constituents, and rarely consult extra-party sources for information and advice on bills.

The causal model (Figure 5.1) assumes the following pattern. Senators who came from urban political environments are usually "upper crust". Directors of firms, lawyers, and non-Catholics very often believe that they got into politics for partisan reasons and that they contribute occupational expertise to legislative review. Most partisan- and expertise-oriented senators say that they are primarily accountable to their party organization, and that they rarely communicate with "constituents" or with ad hoc and attentive publics. Senators with these narrow institutional orientations most strongly prefer business review.

The actual correlations suggest that the assumptions are surprisingly accurate (see Table 5.3). First, the relationships between the proportion of urban population and the socio-economic variables indicate that lawyers and, to a lesser degree, corporate directors come disproportionately from heavily urban centres. Second, the relationships between the socio-economic and the behavioural variables suggest that directors of firms, non-Catholics, and lawyers often attribute their committee work to occupational expertise. Corporation directors often say, too, that they entered politics for partisan reasons and chose their speciality because it is an outgrowth of their occupational experience. Third, the links between behavioural and institutional orientations reveal that many senators who bring their expertise to committee work and who readily point to partisan motives for entering politics also claim that they are accountable mainly to their parties. Finally, the correlations between institutional orientations and senators' choice of business review indicate, in particular, that senators who defer to their party clearly favour business review.

So as to test whether the categories of influences actually relate to one another and to senators' adoption of business review roles in causal sequence, the model *predicts* that no category of influences will have independent affects on variables subsequent to the one it affects directly. We may summarize the predictions as follows:

1. The degree to which a senator's federal constituency of residence is "urban" does not independently affect his behavioural orientations, his institutional orientations, or his choice of business review when we control for his socioeconomic background. (See predictions 1, 2, and 3, Table 5.4.)

2. A senator's socio-economic background does not independently affect his institutional orientations or his choice of business review when we control for his behavioural orientations. (See predictions 4 and 5.)

3. A senator's behavioural orientations do not independently affect his choice of business review when we control for his institutional orientations. The results of tests on these predictions appear in Table 5.4. With one exception (1[3]), those predictions which do not include the variable "business review" are borne out by the small magnitude of the path coefficients. The categories of influences do, then, appear to affect senators' perceptions of business review in causal sequence.

The over-all causal model, therefore, yielded sufficiently robust findings to support strongly the view that senators adopt and develop business-review roles in response to a discernible and coherent pattern of influences on how they perceive their legislative tasks. Senators from urban areas are often directors of firms and lawyers. Directors, lawyers, and non-Catholics in the Upper House often say that their occupational and committee interests coincide. Most directors, moreover, say that they entered politics for partisan reasons, and that they chose their legislative specialities on the basis of expertise. Senators who attribute their committee interests and legislative specialities to occupational expertise and who are in politics for partisan reasons often say that they defer mostly to their party. Senators who defer to their party also say that business review is their most effective channel of influence. The cumulative impact of this sequence of influences gives business reviewers deeply rooted and intense views of their legislative work. In the words of a business reviewer from one of Canada's two main financial centres:

Table 5.4 PREDICTIONS ABOUT THE INTERRELATEDNESS
OF INFLUENCES ON "BUSINESS REVIEW"

Prediction	Path Coefficient
1. $rAC.B=0$	
(1) $rac_1.(b_1b_2b_3)$	$= .12$
(2) $rac_2.(b_1b_2b_3)$	$= .16$
(3) $rac_3.(b_1b_2b_3)$	$= .28^b$
2. $rAD.B=0$	
(1) $rad_1.(b_1b_2b_3)$	$= .07$
(2) $rad_2.(b_1b_2b_3)$	$= .22$
(3) $rad_3.(b_1b_2b_3)$	$= .18$
3. $rAE.B=0$	
(1) $rae.(b_1b_2b_3)$	$= .22$
4. $rBD.C=0$	
(1) $rd_1(b_1b_2b_3).(c_1c_2c_3)$	$= .29$
(2) $rd_2(b_1b_2b_3).(c_1c_2c_3)$	$= .08$
(3) $rd_3(b_1b_2b_3).(d_1d_2d_3)$	$= .11$
5. $rBE.C=0$	
(1) $re(b_1b_2b_3).(c_1c_2c_3)$	$= .49^a$
6. $rCE.D=0$	
(1) $re(c_1c_2c_3).(d_1d_2d_3)$	$= .36^b$

[a]significant at 0.01 level   [b]significant at 0.05 level

I guess you could say that I am a representative of the Anglo-Saxon and business establishment. Ottawa revolves in an orbit almost totally divorced from reality, that is, pressures like having to meet a payroll. As a businessman and tax lawyer, I understand the technical situation which the bureaucrats are trying to address and so I can make reasonable and valid recommendations. My resources are both personal and institutional. First, I rely heavily on my experience in corporate law and help from people in my law firm to thoroughly research suggestions that I have for amendments. Second, I take advantage of my prerogatives as a Senator to talk up my recommendations in caucus and to approach directly the Minister in charge of the bill. I avoid even the appearance of my attacking the Minister or the Government. In fact, I go the low-profile route. I try to press as persuasively as possible the technical arguments which I want to make. I don't have to go public. Certainly, everyone knows I will support the Government when the time comes for a vote. MPs and Ministers usually get the message from the technical arguments. That is, they see that I am saying, "When do you want this legislation passed in the Senate, next month or next year?"

The Interrelatedness of Influences on "Social Investigation"
Figure 5.2 outlines the second causal analysis. It portrays the way in which province characteristics, socio-economic background, behavioural orientations, and institutional orientations combine to influence a senator's choice of social investigation as a legislative role. The selection of variables for the respective categories of influence was based on the following findings:

A. Social investigators usually come from provincial political environments that have the following things in common: they have more representatives, per person, in the Senate than other provinces do; and their parties hold a fairly large plurality of seats in their province's House of Commons delegation.

B. Several socio-economic variables influenced "social investigation". Senators who were born and raised in the Atlantic provinces, and presently represent that area, are strongly inclined toward social investigation. Others who take well to the role are French Canadians, non-lawyers, non-businessmen, and those who received at least part of their education outside of their provinces.

C. Several behavioural orientations influence senators' choice of social investigation. For one, those who say that they selected their favourite committee for altruistic reasons overwhelmingly choose social investigation. Those, moreover, who cite expertise along with altruistic reasons for proposing revisions of legislation also tend to choose the role.

D. Senators who like to act as liaisons for constituents and interest groups in Parliament often choose social investigation. This fact is especially true of members who gather advice and

Figure 5.2 The Interrelatedness of Influences on Social Investigation

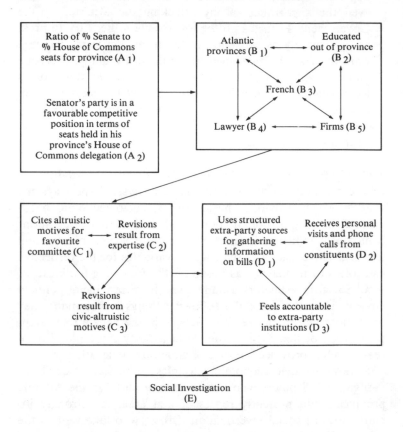

information from these extra-party sources. It is also true of those who make themselves accessible to constituents, being available often to talk on the phone or to receive visitors, and of those who feel that they are accountable to extra-party organizations.

Figure 5.2 assumes that the political environment of a province directly influences the socio-economic backgrounds of those from the area who are selected to be senators. Senators with five socio-economic traits, the figure assumes, will often say that they perform committee work and legislative review from altruistic motives, although they want to apply their expertise as well. Altruistic senators will utilize open institutional strategies, weighing the views of extra-party organizations and communicating with the people back home. These legislators ultimately find a niche in social investigation. The findings from the causal analysis generally fail to support the model. First, the statistics reveal very ambiguous and mostly weak relations between the two province characteristics and the five socio-economic variables (Table 5.5; [1]). They do indicate, however, that those senators who come from provinces which have high *per-capita* representation in the Senate usually were born and raised in, and represent the Atlantic provinces (1[1]). This relationship is partly tautological in that it indicates that the Atlantic provinces are, in any case, the most heavily overrepresented provinces in the Senate.

Second, the statistics reveal some very strong correlations between socio-economic variables and behavioural orientations. Atlantic-provinces senators (2[1]) and non-lawyers (2[4]) both say that they select committees for altruistic reasons. Senators educated outside of their provinces like to apply their expertise when advocating legislative revisions (2[7]). These findings make good sense. Senators from Atlantic Canada and non-lawyers probably believe that their presence adds a human dimension to the Senate; their humbler origins offset the technical emphasis which the rich, urban lawyers place upon legislative review.

Third, the statistics indicate that the relationship between behavioural and institutional orientations is quite weak. There is only one affirmative finding. Senators who like to apply their expertise to revisions are the same legislators who go to extra-party sources for advice and information (3[2]). Senators who claim altruistic motives for pushing revisions, however, generally do not hold themselves accountable to extra-party institutions (3[9]). The negative evidence, therefore, weighs against this segment of the model as being salient.

Finally, we learned (earlier in this chapter) that key institutional orientations do influence "social investigation"; that is,

Table 5.5 ASSUMPTIONS ABOUT THE INTERRELATEDNESS
OF INFLUENCES ON "SOCIAL INVESTIGATION"

Assumption	Pearson's Correlation Coefficient	Expected/Actual Direction of Relation
1. $rAB \neq 0$		
(1) ra_1b_1	$= .90^a$	+/+
(2) ra_2b_1	$= -.15$	+/−
(3) ra_1b_2	$= -.11$	+/−
(4) ra_2b_2	$= .11$	+/+
(5) ra_1b_3	$= -.15$	+/−
(6) ra_2b_3	$= .11$	+/+
(7) ra_1b_4	$= -.19$	−/−
(8) ra_2b_4	$= .16$	−/+
(9) ra_1b_5	$= -.14$	−/−
(10) ra_2b_5	$= .10$	−/+
2. $rBC \neq 0$		
(1) rb_1c_1	$= .25^b$	+/+
(2) rb_2c_1	$= .12$	+/+
(3) rb_3c_1	$= -.08$	+/−
(4) rb_4c_1	$= -.21^b$	−/−
(5) rb_5c_1	$= -.17$	−/−
(6) rb_1c_2	$= .00$	+/+
(7) rb_2c_2	$= .26^b$	+/+
(8) rb_3c_2	$= -.07$	+/−
(9) rb_4c_2	$= .02$	−/+
(10) rb_5c_2	$= -.11$	−/−
(11) rb_1c_3	$= -.01$	+/−
(12) rb_2c_3	$= .11$	+/+
(13) rb_3c_3	$= -.01$	+/−
(14) rb_4c_3	$= .02$	−/+
(15) rb_5c_3	$= .03$	−/+
3. $rCD \neq 0$		
(1) rc_1d_1	$= .14$	+/+
(2) rc_2d_1	$= .21^b$	+/+
(3) rc_3d_1	$= -.05$	+/+
(4) rc_1d_2	$= .04$	+/+
(5) rc_2d_2	$= .13$	+/+
(6) rc_3d_2	$= .10$	+/+
(7) rc_1d_3	$= .10$	+/+
(8) rc_2d_3	$= .02$	+/+
(9) rc_3d_3	$= -.22^b$	+/−
4. $rDE \neq 0$		
(1) rd_1e	$= .26^b(.24)(.27)$	+/+
(2) rd_2e	$= .21^b(.19)(.21)$	+/+
(3) rd_3e	$= .18 (.13)(.16)$	+/+

[a]significant at 0.01 level   [b]significant at 0.05 level

senators who consult extra-party organizations and feel themselves accountable to these groups gravitate toward social investigation, as do members who make themselves available to phone calls and visits from constituents (4). Clearly, the model's assumptions lack explanatory power.

It does not make sense to test whether the various categories of influences interrelate in causal sequence. The correlations between the categories tell us only one thing that we did not already know, namely, that senators from the Atlantic provinces and non-lawyers often attribute their committee preferences to altruistic reasons. We do not find the type of coherent pattern of influences on social investigators' choice of their role that analysis of business reviewers' adoption of their role revealed. Most important, it does not appear that our respondents with altruistic behavioural orientations follow through by developing strong ties with extra-party institutions in an effort to build up a national constituency around their main policy interests. We saw in Chapter 1 that the few successful social investigators, especially Maurice Lamontagne and Keith Davey, were able to translate their issue interests into policy proposals with strong and general appeal outside of their party and Parliament. But, the relatively humble backgrounds of most social investigators should alert us to a lack of sophistication in their ranks. In comparison with business reviewers, most of whom come from Montreal and Toronto, and have a great deal of expertise in business and in corporate law, social investigators become babes-in-the-woods when they accept their appointments and make the trek to Ottawa. In other words, their lack of sophistication has probably contributed greatly to social investigators' relatively poor showing in the recent competition with business reviewers for the benefits of institutionalization.

CONCLUSIONS

This chapter tested the theory that four categories of variables which reflect a senator's past and attitudes will influence each other and that, in turn, they will combine to affect a senator's choice of a legislative role. The model assumed that various political environments (i.e., federal constituencies and provinces) influence the socio-economic characteristics of Senate appointees. Senators with specific social backgrounds are likely to have behavioural orientations and, consequently, institutional orientations which prime them to prefer either business review or social investigation.

The theory passed the test quite well when the four categories of influences were related to the variable "business review". Urban "constituencies", the study showed, provide a relatively large number of senators who are lawyers and/or directors of firms. These two traits are among the socio-economic characteristics which, John Porter maintains, distinguish the upper crust of Canada's elite groups from the lower echelons of the country's power structure.[2] Along the classic lines of liberal democracy in Canada as described by Robert Presthus,[3] the directors, lawyers, *and* non-Catholics mainly say that they are motivated by partisan interests and a desire to put their expertise to work on governmental problems. Their bias is toward big business. Political parties in search of money for election campaigns know this, and realize the value of forming alliances with such senators. As a result they share a sort of mutual understanding. The senators toe a party line just so long as they have the privilege of reviewing legislation on behalf of the business community. When asked about their relations with their party, about the people they represent, and about sub-groups and interests, it is these senators who say that they are accountable to their party and that they rarely communicate with extra-party organizations. Finally, those who defer to their party in this way very often believe that they are successful business reviewers.

Where key variables from the four categories were related to social investigation, however, the theory fell far short of the expectations. We saw that, contrary to Kenneth Prewitt's and Heinz Eulau's findings,[4] senators who were social investigators and thus were particularly attuned to demands for social change did not necessarily come from heavily populated and competitive political environments. Rather, social investigators were more likely to come from the Atlantic provinces, which are overrepresented in the Senate. Social investigators, as well, usually represent provinces where their party is in a relatively safe competitive position. Despite these findings, we wanted to ascertain whether the province characteristics which do relate to "social investigation" influence intervening variables in a causal sequence similar to the pattern of affects on "business review". The results do suggest that the Atlantic-provinces senators very often are long-term residents of their provinces, non-lawyers, and non-directors. The long-term residents and non-lawyers, in turn, often say altruism motivates them to work in their favourite committees. Otherwise, the model indicates very little.

At the outset this chapter suggested that a link exists between the process whereby senators are appointed and the power of business reviewers in the Upper House. As was noted in Chapter 4, the influx of new blood and internal reforms did little to keep business reviewers from gaining more power; indeed, far more than social investigators, business reviewers capitalized on these institutional changes. The study thus asked: Does a snowball effect occur whereby the dominant backgrounds and traits of senators combine to intensify their commitments to business review and, ultimately, the hegemony of the role?

Our findings from the causal model of influence on senators' choice of business review strongly support such an assertion. In addition, the test of a similar model of influences on senators' choice of social investigation suggests that the factors which lead to the development of this role relate to one another much less coherently.

The findings of this chapter suggest that, given the nature of appointments, no amount of tinkering with age limits or internal structure will reduce the oligarchic orientation of the Senate. Business review evolves from the nature of Senate appointments. Some senators lack the credentials or temperament for business review and, thus, do not become members of the lobby from within. These senators can become social investigators. Yet, their choice of social investigation seems to develop as much by default as by choice.

Chapter 6 will probe the data further, especially by comparing them with data from Allan Kornberg's and William Mishler's study of MPs. We have already seen that MPs choose social investigation much more frequently than senators do (Chapter 3). Is that because MPs are elected?

NOTES

1. The analysis employed the regression program available through the Statistical Package for Social Sciences explained in Norman H. Nie *et al., Statistical Package for Social Scientists* (New York, 1970), Chapter 15. The results of stepwise multiple regressions on the key variables are summarized in terms of three statistics. These are: (1) the Correlation Coefficient (r)— the strength of the relationship between the two variables; (2) Beta (weights)—the amount of change in the dependent variable which is produced by a standardized change in one of the independent variables when the others in the equation are controlled; and (3) r Square—the proportion of the variance in the dependent variable accounted for by the regression equation.

2. John Porter, *The Vertical Mosaic: An Analysis of Social Class and Power in Canada* (Toronto, 1965), especially pp. 71, 91, 266, and 386-98.

3. Robert Presthus, *Elite Accommodation in Canadian Politics* (Toronto, 1973), pp. 60-63.

4. Kenneth Prewitt and Heinz Eulau, "Political Matrix and Political Representation: Prolegomenon to a New Departure From an Old Problem", *American Political Science Review*, 63 (June 1969), p. 428.

6. Senators as Compared to MPs: Differences Attributable to Elections

Are MPS more responsive to the demands of a pluralistic society than senators are? Are elected public officeholders more responsive than appointees are? Until Kenneth Prewitt and Heinz Eulau posed the second question,[1] there was a general assumption among students of public officeholders, based on no particular set of data, that electoral processes forced incumbents to be responsive to public demands because their tenure depended upon voters' approval. On the other hand, the assumption went, appointees to public office may act independently of demands from the combination of sub-groups and interests that one must please in order to stay in elective office. Prewitt and Eulau challenged this assumption, encouraging researchers to perform comparative studies of elected and appointed officeholders who work in the same political arena. Since Prewitt and Eulau made this plea, Kornberg's and Mishler's study of MPS has appeared as has this present one of senators. Both studies are based on interview data which were gathered in the same year. These data provide an opportunity for us to test the disputed assumption that elected officeholders are more responsive than appointees. They also permit us to confirm whether or not so many senators choose business review and eschew social investigation because they are appointed.

We do know that MPS are younger, belong more to minority ethnic groups, and have less distinguished careers in business than senators (see Chapter 2). In other words, they do reflect the socio-economic texture of the Canadian people more accurately than do senators. We also know (Chapter 3) that MPs choose social investigation as their role more often than senators. In this chapter, we will attempt to ascertain which influences trigger, or fail to trigger, MPs' relative preference for business review or social investigation, and thereby try to determine whether or not the electoral process is such an influence. The analysis will focus also on the way in which MPs and senators develop institutional orientations. Do they take cues from their parties? Do they attempt to consult extra-party groups and institutions on important legislative problems?

APPOINTED AND ELECTED OFFICEHOLDERS:
SOME POINTERS FROM THE LITERATURE

The issue of the influence of elections on representatives is one of the enduring questions of political science. V. O. Key says that elections set up a relationship between public opinion and the performance of the political elite.[2] Robert A. Dahl adds that elections assure us that politicians who act improperly or unfairly will most likely be found out.[3] Some authors, however, say that these supposed links between public opinion and political performance have little reality. While Dahl says that public officeholders in liberal democracies simply reflect the fundamental values and goals of the general public, empirical surveys have frequently failed to support this belief. Herbert McCloskey, for instance, found that in the United States such consensus is not widespread among the general populace and really exists only among the political leaders.[4]

Researchers have also studied how elections affect legislative output. John G. Grumm cites a number of studies which have shown that variations in the malapportionment of seats in legislatures have little or no predictable effect on policy outputs.[5] In addition, Thomas Dye considered the output of welfare policies and found that party competition by itself has no clear effect on this output.[6] And, of course, there is Prewitt's and Eulau's study of San Francisco Bay Area city councils; they found that "elections do not necessarily remove councils which respond only to their own image of community needs".[7]

Although the present analysis is the first to compare the role perceptions of appointed and elected *legislators*, some previous studies have compared the perceptions of high-level bureaucrats and legislators. The results of these latter studies supported the above findings, which, in turn led Prewitt and Eulau to challenge the assumption that elections make legislators more responsive to pluralistic demands. Roger Davidson, for instance, studied both members of the U.S. House of Representatives and bureaucrats in the U.S. federal government from the standpoint of their responsiveness.[8] He noted that the bureaucrats do respond to demands from certain sectors of society even though they .do not reflect society as a whole in terms of geography and socio-economic background. Such sectors include people (for example, with technical expertise) and industries (such as textile manufacturers or oil producers, which develop clientele relationships with governmental agencies). Very often the most important job a bureaucrat can do is to articulate the diverse claims of pertinent technical and commercial sectors, and to act as a broker for them. Davidson asserts that legislators do this job only in so far as they become specialists.[9]

Robert Presthus's recent study contributes an important perspective to the question of elite responsiveness in Canada.[10] As we saw in Chapter 3, he surveyed the perceptions of interactions among interest-group directors, bureaucrats, and legislators in four Canadian political arenas (the federal government, and the provincial governments of Ontario, Quebec, and British Columbia). Unfortunately, his sample excluded senators. Presthus found that the necessary accommodations between interests often occur between governmental agencies and private political elites without recourse to legislators.[11] It is not surprising then that many MPS report that they are relegated to running a lot of errands for their constituents who have grievances about governmental services (Chapter 2). Many of these errands amount to "small claims" work rather than policy surveillance. While MPS are more responsive to the "little guy" than are high-level bureaucrats, their concern does not as readily translate into influence. Presthus's findings indicate that interest-group directors are aware of this situation.

These observations notwithstanding, some MPs do influence policy because they are adept at the articulation and brokerage of claims on the level of issues. Further, MPs try to influence policy in the direction of social reform more than senators do. To what extent is this due to the fact that MPs are elected?

MEASURES OF ORIENTATIONS TO BUSINESS REVIEW AND
SOCIAL INVESTIGATION

Kornberg and Mishler asked MPs three questions to find out what type of work they were most interested in. Their questions, like those used for the present study, concerned MPs' specialities, the committees to which they belong, and their favourite committees. MPs' responses were coded to correspond to those of senators. Business review specialities were those which related to commerce and finance. The application to these data of factor analysis disclosed that MPs' membership of the Finance, Trade, and Economic Affairs, Miscellaneous Estimates, and Public Accounts committees clustered together in a single group, much as senators' membership of the Banking and National Finance committees did.

Data already reported in Chapter 3 indicate that MPs are much less oriented to business review than are senators. Twenty-two, 23, and 16 per cent of the MPs, respectively, reported specializing in business review, belonging to a related committee, and favouring a business review committee. The comparable figures for senators were 49, 41, and 21 per cent.

Following the tack taken in Chapter 3 with respect to social investigation, factor analysis pooled distributions of senators' and MPs' responses to the three business review questions. Senators, particularly because of the relative strength of the Banking, Trade, and Commerce Committee, have greater access to business review than MPs.[12] An additive measure, based on loadings from factor analysis of MPs' *and* senators' responses, gauges more accurately MPs' involvement in the role as it is generally performed in Parliament.

The pooled responses of the legislators to the three business-review items load well on one factor without rotation.[13] For purposes of comparison, MPs and senators were ascribed forty-six points if business review was their speciality, forty points if they belonged to a related committee, and eighteen points if one of these committees was their favourite. The average score of MPs on this measure (22.45),[14] as compared to that of senators (42.82),[15] indicated the degree to which MPs are less oriented toward business review than are senators.

Chapter 3 reports in detail a similar factor analysis of MPs' and senators' responses to the speciality and committee questions which relate to social investigation. MPs' scores on the resulting additive variable indicate very clearly that they are much more oriented to the role than are senators. Whereas 32 per cent of senators had a score of zero, only 25 per cent of MPs did; and whereas the average senator obtained 37.34 points,[16] the average MP received 57.24.[17]

KEY INFLUENCES ON MPs' PERCEPTIONS OF LEGISLATIVE ROLES
Business Review
We might expect MPs who are business reviewers to share many characteristics with their counterparts in the Senate. That is, we might expect them to come mainly from densely populated constituencies, to be members of the socio-economic upper crust, to attribute their political and legislative activities to partisan and occupational motives, and to claim that they are accountable to their party and are relatively free of extra-party pressures.

With a few exceptions, the test of these expectations (Table 6.1) used the same variables within the categories of influences here as were used in Chapter 5. But because MPs hold few directorships and have rarely held other federal public offices, the test excluded these variables from the social- and political-background categories. Also, since Kornberg and Mishler did not ask MPs why they chose their favourite committee or why they had pressed for revisions of bills, the test (on MPs' behavioural-orientation variables) omitted four measures which appeared in the analysis of senators' orientations: (1) "attributes choice of favourite committee to (a) altruism, (b) occupational expertise"; and (2) "revisions motivated by (a) altruism, (b) occupational expertise".

Table 6.1 "BUSINESS REVIEW" REGRESSED ON . . . FOR MPS

Variables	Correlation Coefficient (Simple r)	Normalized Regression Coefficient (Beta Score)	Multiple Regression Coefficient (r Square)
1. a. Constituency			
i) % of vote for Progressive Conservatives	.15[b]	.15[b]	.02[b]
b. Province			
i) % of population urban	—.20[a]	—.20[a]	.04[a]
ii) Proportion of seats in the Senate in relation to population	.20[a]	.11	.05[b]
2. a. Social Background			
i) # of parents born in Canada	—.16[b]	—.16[b]	.02[b]
ii) Born, raised in, and represents Atlantic provinces	.15[b]	.17[b]	.05[a]
iii) Businessman	.14	.13	.07[a]
iv) Raised in a city	—.11	—.11	.08[a]
b. Political Background			
i) Liberal	—.20[a]	—.20[a]	.04[a]
ii) Has held public office on local level	.19[a]	.16[b]	.07[a]
iii) Holds leadership position in Parliament	.08	.15[b]	.09[a]
iv) Tenure	—.07	—.13	.10[a]
3. Behavioural Orientations			
i) Attributes speciality to altruistic motives	.15[b]	.16[b]	.02[b]
ii) Contacts Cabinet Ministers about constituency matters	.15[b]	.15[b]	.05[b]
iii) Got into politics as result of upbringing	.14	.12	.06[a]
iv) Got into politics for partisan reasons	.14	.09	.07[a]
4. Institutional Orientations			
i) Feels accountable to party	.58[a]	.58[a]	.34[a]
ii) Expansive in responsiveness and accountability	.00	—.12[b]	.35[a]
iii) Purposive role, constituency service	.01	.10	.36[a]

[a]significant at 0.01 level   [b]significant at 0.05 level

The actual test of the influence of political-environment (constituency and province), social- and political-background, behavioural-orientation, and institutional-orientation variables on MPs' perceptions of business review presents some substantially different relations from those found in the Senate data. Table 6.1 summarizes the significant findings.

Political Environment The findings show that, (1) MPs from constituencies which heavily supported the Progressive Conservative party strongly prefer business review; and (2) MPs from rural provinces which are overrepresented in the Senate strongly prefer the role. These two results seem paradoxical in view of the Atlantic-provinces senators' proclivity for social investigation. Three Atlantic provinces (Newfoundland, P.E.I., and Nova Scotia) are the only areas which were both strongly Conservative in the 1968 election and which are overrepresented in the Senate today.

Social and Political Background The findings on the *social* background variables support the expectation that business reviewers in the House of Commons are mainly from the Atlantic provinces. In addition, MPs whose parents were born outside Canada tend to become business reviewers. Finally, there is an indication that business reviewers are businessmen.

The test of the relation between MPs' *political* backgrounds and their adoption of business-review role perceptions produced some very clear results. Liberal MPs indicated a strong aversion to the role. MPs who previously held local offices and presently hold leadership positions in Parliament (e.g., committee chairmanships) often adopt the role. These findings suggest that party affiliation and political experience influence the development of orientations toward business review.

Behavioural Orientations The findings from testing the relation of MPs' behavioural orientations to their business-review orientation differ sharply from the findings for senators. MPs who attribute their speciality to altruistic motives and who report that they contact Cabinet Ministers about constituency rather than policy matters strongly prefer the role. These findings contrast with the previous findings that partisan and occupational motives related most strongly to senators' perceptions of the role.

Institutional Orientations Only the institutional orientations of MPs who are business reviewers clearly correspond to what was expected on the basis of the Senate data. MPs who say that they are accountable above all to their party overwhelmingly opt for the role. There is also some indication that MPs who limit the number of groups and institutions to which they are responsive and accountable prefer business review.

In sum, we see that the influences on MPs' choice of business review in most respects differ sharply from the influences on senators' choice of the role. For MPs a clear link exists between rural conservatism and business review. The finding that these MPs often are first-generation Canadians, from the Atlantic provinces, and/or give their occupation as "businessman" suggests that they are largely upward mobiles, perhaps small-town entrepreneurs. They are fairly experienced politically, in that they frequently held local public offices before coming to Ottawa and are leaders in Parliament. The business reviewers cite altruistic motives for their legislative involvement, and run many errands to Cabinet Ministers for their constituents. Most important, business reviewers often turn to their parties rather than to other extra-parliamentary organizations for information and cues concerning their actions.

Social Investigation

Judging from data available on the Senate, we might expect that MPs who become social investigators come from non-urban areas, especially from the Atlantic provinces, belong to less elite socio-economic groups, cite altruistic interests and occupational expertise as motives for their behaviour, and say they are responsive to groups outside of Parliament. Tests of the relation between the four categories of influences and MPs' perceptions of social investigatory roles mostly supported the predictions (see Table 6.2).

Political Environment MPs from relatively non-urban constituencies and/or those who won by very close margins in 1968 strongly prefer the role. These findings suggest that Prewitt's and Eulau's assumption—that population density intensifies legislators' responsiveness to pluralistic social demands —does not apply to Canadian federal politics. However, the

Table 6.2 "SOCIAL INVESTIGATION" REGRESSED ON . . .

FOR MPS

Variables	Correlation Coefficient (Simple r)	Normalized Regression Coefficient (Beta Score)	Multiple Regression Coefficient (r Square)
1. a. Constituency			
i) % of population urban	−.25[a]	−.25[a]	.06[a]
ii) Difference between % of vote for the winning and second strongest party	−.21[a]	−.17[b]	.09[a]
iii) # of ethnic groups in the area	−.08	−.08	.10[a]
b. Province			
i) Population of the province	−.16[b]	−.16[b]	.03[b]
2. Background			
a. Social			
i) Lawyer	−.35[a]	−.35[a]	.12[a]
ii) Other than Anglo-Saxon or French	.13	.14[b]	.14[a]
iii) Raised in a city	−.20[a]	−.17[b]	.17[a]
iv) Age	−.09	−.11	.18[a]
v) Educational attainment	−.29[a]	−.16	.20[a]
b. Political			
i) Holds a leadership position in parliamentary party organization	−.38[a]	−.38[a]	.14[a]
ii) Has held party offices on the local level	−.20[a]	−.15[b]	.17[a]
iii) Has held public office on the local level	.17[b]	.12	.18[a]
3. Behavioural Orientations			
i) Contacts Cabinet Ministers about constituency matters	.31[a]	.31[a]	.10[a]
ii) Attributes speciality to political experiences	−.23[a]	−.21[a]	.14[a]
4. Institutional Orientations			
i) Rates party sources highly for advice on bills	−.15[b]	−.15[b]	.02[b]
ii) Rates extra-party structures highly for advice on bills	.12	.17[b]	.05[b]
iii) Communication with constituents mainly concerns governmental services	−.14	−.16	.07[b]

[a]significant at 0.01 level   [b]significant at 0.05 level

findings do support their assertion that competition in political environments appreciably affects legislators' interest in social demands.

The principal findings on the political environments in MPs' provinces reinforce this observation. MPs from provinces with small populations show a strong propensity for social investigation. The pluralistic social demands of urban centres notwithstanding, it appears that MPs are especially inclined toward social legislation if they come from a relatively non-urban province in which electoral competition is intense.

Social Background Non-lawyers, members of ethnic groups other than Anglo-Saxon and French, and non-urban-raised MPs all tend to become social investigators. There is also some evidence that those MPs with relatively low educational attainment become involved in the role. These findings are particularly important in view of the fact that MPs reflect the texture of Canadian society, with respect to the above characteristics, much better than do senators. We see then that MPs with more representative background characteristics translate their experiences into concerns with social reform.

Political Background MPs who have not yet attained high positions in their party organizations tend to prefer social investigation. That is, social investigators usually have not held party offices on the local level or in their party's parliamentary organization.

Behavioural Orientations Social investigators frequently contact Cabinet Ministers about their constituents' problems with governmental services, rather than about policy questions; also, they rarely say that they got into social investigation because of political experience.

Institutional Orientations MPs who rarely seek advice from party sources and who extensively consult other groups and institutions prefer the role. These findings contrast sharply with those on the mainly party-oriented business reviewers. Social investigators, in addition, do not feel that they are overburdened by constituents' service requests, even though they try to respond to a lot of these small claims.

By way of comparison, then, MPs who are social investigators share some traits with their colleagues who are business reviewers. They both come from underpopulated constituencies, they both represent some disadvantaged sectors of Canadian life, and they both approach Cabinet Ministers mainly about constituents' problems with the administration of policies. In some respects, however, they differ sharply from each other. Social investigators are relatively inexperienced in party leadership and come from much more competitive constituencies than business reviewers do. Their apparent reluctance to take cues from their party and their eagerness to consult other sources for advice also distinguish them from business reviewers.

A comparison of influences on senators' and MPS' accountability and responsiveness to extra-party structures might contribute a valuable perspective on whether or not electoral processes affect legislators' behaviour. The finding, for instance, that competitive political environments engender communication with extra-party organizations among MPS but not among senators would contribute greatly to our understanding of the linkage between various publics and their representatives.

KEY FACTORS WHICH INFLUENCE SENATORS' AND MPS'
RESPONSIVENESS TO EXTRA-PARTY ORGANIZATIONS

Senators who are social investigators usually gather information on bills from structured extra-party sources, often receive personal visits and phone calls, and seldom feel especially accountable to their party. MPS who are social investigators, similarly, frequently consult extra-party structures for information on bills, avoid party sources, and often say that their constituents communicate about matters other than service requests. In short, social investigators in both the Senate and the House claim that they are responsive to the policy needs of their various publics.

Two additive variables measure how senators and MPS respond to the views of these publics. Senators who consult extra-party sources of information, receive personal calls and visits, or say that they feel accountable to extra-party structures were given twenty-four, seventeen, and seventeen points for respective responses.[18] MPS who eschew party sources of information, consult extra-party structures, and engage in communication which concerns other than constituency service

Table 6.3 KEY INFLUENCES ON SENATORS' AND MPS' RESPONSIVENESS TO OUTSIDE GROUPS AND INSTITUTIONS

Senators' Information and Communication

Regressed on	Correlation Coefficient (r)	Beta at Entry (Normalized Regression Coefficient)	r Square
Background Variables			
A. "Constituency"			
1. % of population urban	-.41a	-.41a	.17a
2. % of votes for Social Credits	.22	.19	.20a
3. % of vote for 1st party minus 2nd party	-.06	.14	.22a
B. Province			
1. Population	-.27b	-.27b	.08b
2. % of vote for NDP	-.15	-.09	.08
3. % of vote for Liberals	-.18	-.15	.09

MPs' Information and Communication

Regressed on	Correlation Coefficient (r)	Beta at Entry (Normalized Regression Coefficient)	r Square
Background Variables			
A. Constituency			
1. % of population urban	-.20a	-.20a	.04a
2. % of vote that went to parties other than Liberal, PC, NDP, or SC	.19a	.18a	.07a
3. % of voter turnout in 1968	-.15b	-.14b	.09a
B. Province			
1. Near perfect competition in votes received by parties	-.11	-.11	.01
2. % of Senate Seats/ % of House Seats	-.04	-.10	.02
3. % of population urban	-.08	-.24b	.05b

C. Social

1. Raised in city	−.30[a]	−.30[a]	.09[a]
2. Born, raised in, and represents Atlantic provinces	−.29[b]	.19	.12[b]
3. Age	−.06	.16	.14[b]

D. Political

1. Held public office on provincial level	.28[b]	.28[b]	.08[b]
2. Has held party offices on local level	.23[b]	.23[b]	.13[a]
3. Unsuccessful candidate for federal office	.20	.18	.17[a]

Behavioural Orientations

1. Purposive role—policy	−.20	−.20	.04
2. Stays in politics because of political influence he/she can have	.12	.23	.08[b]
3. Being a senator is his/her main occupation	−.12	−.18	.11[b]

C. Social

1. Educated out of province	−.25[a]	−.25[a]	.06[a]
2. Lawyer	−.17[b]	−.16[b]	.09[a]
3. Protestant	−.13	−.11	.10[a]

D. Political

1. Unsuccessful candidate in federal campaign	−.16[b]	−.16[b]	.02[b]
2. Unsuccessful candidate in provincial campaign	.09	.11	.03[b]
3. Has held party offices on all levels	−.11	−.12	.05[b]

Behavioural Orientations

1. Attributes legislative speciality to political experience	−.10	−.10	.01
2. Stays in politics for civic-altruistic motives	.07	.08	.02
3. Contacts Cabinet Ministers to represent constituency matters	.08	.07	.02

[a] significant at 0.01 level

[b] significant at 0.05 level

matters obtained, respectively, nineteen, nineteen, and sixteen points.[19] The various points were derived from the coefficients from testing the relation of senators' and MPs' institutional orientations and perceptions of roles in social investigation, respectively (Tables 5.2 and 6.2).

The tests of the relation between the characteristics of senators' and MPs' federal constituencies and their responsiveness reveal that responsive MPs often come from areas which gave relatively strong support to candidates other than the Liberal, PC, NDP, or Social Credit. Among both senators and MPs, those from relatively rural federal constituencies are the most likely to say that they are responsive. Senators from provinces with small and rural populations also tend to say that they are responsive. Prewitt's and Eulau's assertion that responsive legislators are most likely to come from urban areas, thus, does not find support in these findings. MPs, moreover, appear to be no more inclined to choose a responsive style than senators if their riding or province political environment is competitive.

The tests of the relation between senators' and MPs' social backgrounds and their responsiveness reveal two different arrays of influences. First, responsive senators tend to be "country cousins"; they frequently were raised outside of cities, and often have lived all their lives in the Atlantic provinces. Second, responsive MPs had relatively modest backgrounds in that they were educated in their provinces and were not lawyers. The extent to which the Prime Minister must appoint senators from the Atlantic provinces, therefore, contributes to the Senate's responsiveness. Voters tend to select MPs who have modest backgrounds relative to senators; and this contributes to the number of MPs who choose responsive styles.

With respect to political background, responsive senators and MPs both have had successful political careers. Responsive senators have often held local and provincial offices; responsive MPs have hardly ever lost an election. Since responsive senators and MPs are both politically experienced, we cannot conclude that dependence on public approval for re-election alone triggers responsiveness in legislators. That is, many senators do not abandon career-long styles of response once they win appointment to the Upper House.

Finally, the responsiveness measures were regressed on senators' and MPS' behavioural orientations. In neither group are the results statistically significant.

CONCLUSIONS

In this chapter a number of interesting differences and similarities between senators and MPS became apparent. First, we recalled that Senate business reviewers are "city cats" with extremely close ties to the business community; they say, moreover, that they articulate and accommodate the business point of view. House-of-Commons business reviewers, on the other hand, appear to be small-town businessmen, mainly from Progressive-Conservative areas. Rather than articulating the business point of view in the policy process, they register constituents' complaints about governmental services. These findings point up one profound problem with the role of elections in maintaining ties between representatives and the business community. Although business-review MPS might represent small businesses rather than large firms, the Senate business reviewers are more likely to have the contacts and the expertise necessary to accommodate governmental policy to the business viewpoint.

Unlike Senate and House-of-Commons business reviewers, social investigators share similar characteristics. Generally, both groups are from relatively non-urban constituencies and provinces, especially the Atlantic provinces, both are more socio-economically representative of the general populace than business reviewers, and both are responsive to non-partisan groups and institutions. Since MPS are more representative of the general populace than are senators, they are also more likely to be enthusiastic social investigators. If MPS are exposed to competitive elections, they tend to focus their choice even more sharply on social investigation.

The clearest similarity between senators and MPS is the tendency of social investigators in both groups to prefer extra-party sources of information to intra-party sources. We have already noted the extent to which political scholars view such responsiveness as pivotal to the process whereby pluralistic demands are accommodated in legislatures. Prewitt and Eulau even suggest that, if a legislator is to be responsive, he must come from a highly populated area where elections are competitive. Among senators and MPs, however, those from less-populated and less-urban areas and those with relatively modest socio-economic backgrounds are most responsive. It appears then that responsiveness has social roots at least in Canada's Parliament. Senators and MPs from less-populated and less-urbanized areas, presumably, know their constituents on a more personal basis and so are more likely to share experiences with them.

In sum, elections produce MPs who have different backgrounds, viewpoints, and interests from appointed senators. The apportionment of constituencies assures that MPs come from less urban areas, and that voters choose members who are more representative of the population on a socio-economic level. The Prime Minister, on the other hand, summons people to the Senate who are much less representative of society. Although competitive elections do not appear to make MPs more responsive to structured sources of information on bills, elections do produce MPs who focus their attention more clearly on social issues. Presumably, only elections would provide similarly oriented senators in sufficient numbers to redress the imbalance between business review and social investigation in the Upper House.

NOTES

1. Kenneth Prewitt and Heinz Eulau, "Political Matrix and Political Representation: Prolegomenon to a New Departure from an Old Problem", *American Political Science Review*, 63 (June 1969), p. 433.
2. V. O. Key, *Public Opinion and American Democracy* (New York, 1964), p. 412.
3. Robert A. Dahl, *Who Governs?* (New Haven, Conn., 1961), p. 325.

4. Herbert McCloskey, "Consensus and Ideology in American Politics", *American Political Science Review,* 58 (June 1964), pp. 361-82.
5. John G. Grumm, "Structural Determinants of Legislative Behavior", in Allan Kornberg and Lloyd D. Musolf (eds.), *Legislatures in Developmental Perspective* (Durham, N.C., 1970), pp. 433-41.
6. Thomas Dye, *Politics, Economics, and the Public* (New York, 1966), p. 258.
7. Prewitt and Eulau, "Political Matrix and Political Representation".
8. Roger Davidson, "Congress and the Executive", in Alfred de Grazia (ed.), *Congress: The First Branch of Government* (New York, 1967), p. 400. See also, Dean Mann, "The Selection of Federal Political Executives", *American Political Science Review,* 58 (March 1964), pp. 81-99.
9. Davidson, "Congress and the Executive", p. 408.
10. Robert Presthus, *Elite Accommodation in Canadian Politics* (Toronto, 1973).
11. Ibid., pp. 9, 211, 213, 226.
12. Besides Chapter 1 of this book, see A. D. Doerr, "The Role of White Papers", in G. Bruce Doern and Peter Aucoin (eds.), *The Structure of Policy Making in Canada* (Toronto, 1971), p. 189.
13. The reliability, validity, and invalidity of the resulting additive variables are, respectively, 0.66, 0.82, and 0.01. See note 13 in Chapter 3 for a definition of these terms.
14. Standard deviation, 31.61.
15. Standard deviation, 45.03.
16. Standard deviation, 36.72.
17. Standard deviation, 45.69.
18. Mean, 49.05; standard deviation, 20.75.
19. Mean, 43.29; standard deviation, 16.86.

7.   Conclusions and a Design for Abolition

The findings of this study have lent considerable support to the view, set out in Chapter 1, that the Senate should be abolished. Is abolition, however, a feasible alternative to the present state of parliamentary affairs? This chapter will summarize our key findings to underline how they support the abolitionist position and then consider the question of feasibility. In tackling the latter issue, it will ask four critical questions: (1) How might abolition be accomplished? (2) What obstacles stand in its way? (3) How would it affect the political system as a whole? (4) What type of institution might replace the Senate? This chapter suggests that a permanent provincial conference, or a "House of Provinces" should replace the Senate. A revised constitution, furthermore, should establish such a legislature to assure the provinces participation in formulation of federal policies.

CONCLUSIONS

Chapter 1 laid the groundwork for this study. The chapter began by appraising the Senate's role in Parliament from 1867 to the present. A review of the Confederation Debates told us that the Founding Fathers set up the Senate to perform two tasks. First, it was to keep a conservative eye on the elective House of Commons, in order to safeguard propertied interests. This function we call "oligarchic". Second, it was to defend particular minority interests—provincial or regional—that the elected House might threaten. The British North America Act (1867) gave the Senate veto power over all legislation the House of Commons might pass. Nevertheless, the Upper House rarely employs its veto power, and has not lived up to the expectations of the Founding Fathers. Only very rarely has it significantly protected provincial and regional interests; rather it has functioned mostly oligarchically, protecting propertied interests against potentially "harmful" action by the House of Commons. The Senate primarily protects the interests of major business and financial concerns. To do this it regularly challenges, delays, and at times amends or deletes legislative provisions that might endanger major business and financial concerns, or might overlook "good" business practice. This role is called "business review".

In addition to business review, the Senate, especially during the late 1960s and early 1970s, has performed a second role which would surprise the Founding Fathers. It has undertaken to investigate social problems, and frequently has proposed policy alternatives that the government might adopt to ameliorate these problems. This role reflects Canadians' concern of late with social abuses and systemic problems. This second Senate role is called "social investigation". We noted that the role currently encounters stiff resistance from the Senate leadership and from business reviewers who have denied several maverick senators funds and committee time for special studies.

Chapter 1 then discussed how and why the Senate has steadfastly resisted most efforts to reform it from within, especially those designed to bring greater balance to its role. Two reasons best explain such resistance. First, the Upper House as it now exists provides a reliable setting wherein business review can take place. Business review makes accommodations between the political and business elite, and thus advances the political fortunes of any government. Even after frustrating Senate intervention and delay, governments still choose to support the Senate status quo. Second, the Senate's structure helps business reviewers maintain their dominance of the Upper House. Since business review works primarily to protect business and financial interests, it is really a lobby from within. As such it fulfils the role of the Senate as a bastion of oligarchy in the federal arena; that is, it perpetuates the dominance of special interests in the policy process. As long as the Senate remains essentially oligarchic, maverick senators will be frustrated in their attempts to respond to communities other than business and finance.

Finally, Chapter 1 asked the central question of this study: by encouraging the lobby from within, does the Senate violate a fundamental tenet of liberal democracy? This tenet states that all sectors of a society should enjoy reasonably equal access to governmental decision makers. If the appointment of senators indeed perpetuates the lobby from within, it was suggested, then abolition of the Senate may well be a reasonable consideration.

Chapter 2 focused on senators' geographical constituencies, socio-economic and political backgrounds, behavioural orientations, and institutional orientations. This analysis revealed that many senators come from the elite communities of both business and politics. We found that Prime Minister Trudeau has appointed people to the Senate (1968-74) who are often former public officeholders, Liberal party operatives, and/or business notables. In other words, he has appointed people who are the cream of the political and/or business communities. Such senators differ from MPs in three main ways. (1) They more often come from the populous urban areas within their provinces. (2) They have much more experience in both politics and business. (3) They see themselves as "specialists" who contribute occupational expertise to legislative review, and they do not identify closely with their geographic constituents. They see themselves, in other words, as statesmen, above provincial and regional concerns, who make sure that laws protect the business community and, in turn, the economic well-being of the country.

Chapter 3 discussed how business reviewers work within the Senate. It then introduced social investigators as recent rivals to business reviewers, and looked at how they go about their jobs. It showed that business reviewers find considerable support for their style of work in Canadian liberal democracy. Called "elite accommodation", this style arranges private mediations (rather than public debates) for disputes between leaders of various sectors of society. The numerous cultural and regional differences within the country demand such a style. Yet, elite accommodation favours the business elite; that is, it gives it greater access to the decision-making process than any other sector of Canadian society enjoys. This bias results from the strong ties in the nation between the political and business elite.

Chapter 3 thus focused on the ways in which senators, as members of both the political and business elite, act as liaisons between the two communities. First, they employ their personal contacts in these two worlds to pressure civil servants, Cabinet Ministers, and MPs to formulate and promote amendments to government bills which will protect the business community. Second, they employ Senate committees, especially the Banking, Trade, and Commerce Committee to conduct clause-by-clause studies of key bills. Those senators who combine personal pressure with diligent work on business review committees are most often noticed for their influence in business-related matters by other members of the Ottawa elite groups.

During the late 1960s and early 1970s, the Senate's social investigation had an impact on legislation which rivalled that of business review. Yet social investigators today find themselves in a difficult position. For one thing, they do not enjoy the number or type of elite contacts that business reviewers do. Second, their principal vehicles for investigation—special committees—do not enjoy the permanence and prestige that standing business-review committees do. Thus, social investigators often must travel the country to rally support for their proposals, or press for debates in the Senate to keep an issue alive in Parliament. Many members of the Ottawa elite, nevertheless, say that social investigators have had an important impact on the policy process. The principal advantage business reviewers have over social investigators, then, is that they have been able to institutionalize their role. That is, they have given it a resilience which is firmly rooted in the specific privileges and powers of the Senate.

Chapter 4 explained that the Senate, in response to intense criticism during the 1960s, revamped its institutional structure to strengthen business review and social investigation. Using Nelson Polsby's conceptual framework, it evaluated how much and how well the Senate has institutionalized, especially since

1950. It focused on changes in Senate boundaries, organizational complexity, and internal decision making. With respect to boundaries, senators have at their disposal many amenities and privileges, including a good salary, office space, expense accounts, and research and secretarial assistance. On the negative side of the ledger, new appointees owe their positions to one man, the Prime Minister. Similarly, leaders within the Upper House can usually thank the Prime Minister and/or the Senate's Government Leader for putting them in office. With respect to complexity, senators make collective claims upon resources such as staff assistance and operational facilities; these rival, in terms of expense, those of MPs. Senators have been astute at using these resources to bolster committee studies of legislation. With respect to internal decision making, senators spend a fairly large amount of time discussing procedural matters, and they have introduced rigorous review of their own budget. The Government Leader, however, often introduces an element of favouritism when committee leaderships, investigations, and research funds are being assigned. The most consistent beneficiaries of this favouritism have been business reviewers.

In the late 1960s and early 1970s, it appeared as if social investigators were going to be the principal beneficiaries of Senate institutionalization. Enterprising social investigators such as Senators David Croll, Maurice Lamontagne, and Keith Davey marshalled very considerable resources and ran powerful special committees. But the surge of activity was short-lived. Since then social investigation has been tamed by the Senate leadership. Much of it currently occurs under the aegis of one committee, Legal and Constitutional Affairs, and some enterprising senators have had extreme difficulty winning mandates for studies. Business reviewers, on the other hand, have actually improved the Banking, Trade, and Commerce and National Finance committees as forums for their work. At first, then, it seemed that social investigators were making the Senate's legislative role less oligarchic. In the long run, however, they have barely made a dent in the institutional armour of business review.

Chapter 5 asked if business reviewers dominate the Senate

because the Upper House is an appointive legislature. This question is crucial. Some reform proposals recommended that the retirement age for senators be lowered. Others suggested that western provinces should be given more seats, and/or that all provinces should appoint senators. But these proposals fail to strike at the heart of the Senate's oligarchic nature. That is, Prime Ministers continue to appoint partisan, political, and business notables to the Senate, no matter which sectors of Canadian society are in need of representation. It is not likely that this pattern will change, even as senators retire earlier and leave more vacancies. Further, we might expect most Premiers to send the same types of people to the Senate as Prime Ministers do. Presumably, partisan, political, and business notables are just as visible to Premiers as they are to Prime Ministers.

Chapter 2 indicated that the appointment process selects senators who are urban, have extensive experience in politics and business, describe their role as lending occupational expertise to legislative review, and do not identify with or represent geographic "constituents". The analysis in Chapter 5 predicted that these traits relate to one another so as to reinforce senators' preference for business review. Senators from urban areas tend especially to be business notables; business notables usually attribute their actions to occupational expertise and party loyalty; expertise and party-oriented senators report relatively little communication with sub-groups and interests; and, finally, senators who avoid contact with such outsiders overwhelmingly emphasize business review as a legislative role. Actual causal analysis bore out these expectations. Taken together, the influences on senators' choice of business review reveal a remarkable coherence.

The analysis searched for a comparable coherence in the factors which influence senators' preferences for social investigation. As was shown, social investigators disproportionately: (1) represent relatively non-urban and non-competitive areas; (2) are non-lawyers who have resided for many years in the Atlantic provinces and who were educated out of province; (3) register altruistic motives for their legislative activity; and (4) view themselves as responsive and accountable to sub-groups and interests. Causal analysis, however, suggested that these factors do not interrelate in as coherent a way as influences on senators' choice of business review did. Notably weak was the linkage between senators' giving altruistic behavioural motives and their viewing themselves as accountable to sub-groups and interests. Senators with relatively rural roots and modest socio-economic backgrounds, then, might well choose social investigation by default. That is, their rural roots and modest backgrounds do not translate readily into conscious pursuit of altruistic goals and, in turn, into the type of accountability to sub-groups and interests which intensifies a preference for social investigation.

In sum, Chapter 5 points up that those senators with rural and modest pasts do not adopt social investigation in as calculated and determined a way as senators with urban, socio-economic-elite pasts choose business review. The aptitudes and single-mindedness of business reviewers permitted them ultimately to capitalize on the push to institutionalize the Senate. The influences on business reviewers' role preferences are sustained ultimately by biases in the appointment process.

By way of comparison, Chapter 6 focused on the key influences on MPs' legislative role perceptions. The analysis attempted to ascertain the degree to which the appointment process discourages senators from choosing social investigation. Chapter 6 assumed that MPs would greatly prefer social investigation to business review because of electoral pressures and because they are more socio-economically akin to the general populace than senators are. The actual analysis supported this expectation. MPs do say that they perform business review less often than senators and social investigation more often than senators.

The chapter went on to test the hypothesis that Senate and House-of-Commons business reviewers are mainly from non-competitive urban constituencies. In other words, they are business notables who wish to lend expertise to policy and who generally decide matters without referring to a cross-section of sub-groups and interests. The chapter also predicted that social investigators come mainly from competitive urban constituencies. In other words, they are career politicians who bring altruistic motives to their work and who build national constituencies around issues by consulting cross-sections of subgroups and interests. An analysis was performed of key influences on MPS' choice of roles. Its results did not support the hypotheses.

The political-environment, social- and political-background, behavioural- and institutional-orientation influences on MPS' perceptions of the two roles indicate that MPS who are business reviewers mainly (a) come from federal constituencies which gave strong support to the Progressive Conservative party and from provinces which are relatively non-urban; (b) are long-term residents of the Atlantic provinces, have parents who were not born in Canada, are non-Liberals experienced in local public office, and/or are present leaders in Parliament (e.g., committee chairmen); (c) give altruistic motives for their legislative specialities and say that they contact Cabinet Ministers to discuss constituency matters; and (d) believe that they are most accountable to their party, maintaining that they are accountable and responsive to only a narrow spectrum of sub-groups and interests.

On the other hand, MPS who are social investigators often (a) come from relatively non-urban constituencies which they won by narrow margins; (b) were raised in cities, are not lawyers, are not of British or French descent, and lack leadership experience—whether it be in local public offices, party offices, or in their parliamentary party organizations; (c) attribute contacts with Cabinet Ministers to constituency problems; and (d) rarely consult party sources for advice and information, relying instead on representations from sub-groups and interests on policy questions.

Business reviewers and social investigators in the House of Commons unexpectedly share similar social and political backgrounds and behavioural orientations. As well, both often come from non-urban constituencies. Perhaps MPS from relatively urban constituencies become involved in party-leadership and Cabinet roles which obviate the necessity of developing a legislative speciality.

Social-investigation MPS represent competitive constituencies much more frequently than business-review MPs do. Social investigators, in addition, believe that they are much less reliant upon their parties and much more dependent upon sub-groups and interests for good advice and information on policy issues. *The critical difference, then, between* MPs *who choose one or the other of the two roles is that social investigators are under much greater electoral pressures and, therefore, often augment the advice and information that they receive through party channels with the viewpoints of other sub-groups and interests.*

The way in which MPs become social investigators sheds light on the way in which senators adopt the role. If senators were elected, the findings indicate, their interest in social investigation would evolve less from their relatively rural origins than from partisan competition in those rural ridings' political environments. As we have seen, senators from rural areas come to the role partially by default. That is, their colleagues from urban centres have first call on business-review positions. In other words, even if provinces gain the power to appoint some senators, and Premiers do select incumbents with relatively rural and modest backgrounds, one crucial ingredient for making the Senate less oligarchic would still be missing. That is, senators would still have no obligation to air their beliefs and justify their actions in partisan electoral competition. Without the added mandate from the "folks back home", they would probably remain on the periphery of an Upper House which is dominated by the urban socio-economic elite. Thus we see that our analysis strongly supports our hypothesis: most reform proposals have failed to strike at the heart of the problem, the Senate's oligarchic style.

What then do the facts indicate? If one takes liberal democracy seriously, one cannot condone the current lobby from within. An elected Senate, on the other hand, would fit neither our parliamentary system of government nor our present federal-provincial machinery. For the parliamentary system, in which the government is responsible only to the House of Commons, an elected Senate would provide risks of deadlock between the Upper and Lower Houses such as that which occurred in Australia in 1975. As for its federal function, assuming that the provinces would still receive weighted representation, an elected Senate would carry only a weak echo of many disputes which would continue to be waged mostly in federal-provincial conferences. The only other alternative, therefore, seems to be abolition. Other existing institutions should, of course, be strengthened so as to compensate for loss of the Upper House.

A DESIGN FOR ABOLITION

As Canadians decide whether their country can do without an entire province—Quebec—the suggestion that they can do without the Senate probably comes as less of a shock than it would have even five years ago. The abolition option is a real one. While Canadians are in the throes of debates over their country's survival, they cannot afford to ignore the option just because it would involve fundamental changes in our system. This section explores abolition as a viable option and looks at the obstacles to it; its possible systemic consequences; a scenario by which it might take place; and a proposal for a House of Provinces.

Abolition proposes a fundamental change in the British North America Act. As such it automatically comes up against one obstacle. Any amendments relating to the provinces must by convention receive unanimous agreement by the provinces and, by statute, be referred to the British Parliament. This is because the federal government and the provinces, still, after practically two decades of negotiations, have not agreed upon terms for patriation of the BNA Act (that is, the Canadian Parliament has not passed a constitution to replace that enacted in 1867 by the British Parliament). Such a constitution would provide an entirely domestic formula for amendments which affect provincial powers and rights. Since 1964, the federal government has avoided reliance on the U.K. Parliament and, therefore, has not even attempted to amend the BNA Act on matters regarding the provinces. Since specific numbers of seats in the Senate are allocated to provinces, abolition clearly falls within the compass of actions for which the federal government, by convention, would seek unanimous provincial consent. Senate abolition, then, is not likely to occur apart from patriation of the BNA Act and accompanying constitutional reforms.

Another obstacle to Senate abolition is the federal government's reluctance to initiate such a radical step. We saw in Chapter 1 that the Liberal government proposed some Senate reforms during the federal-provincial conferences of 1968-71. In a letter to provincial Premiers (January 19, 1977), Prime Minister Trudeau presented a package of proposals designed to lure the Premiers to agreement on patriation of the BNA Act. This package included an expanded Senate, with greater representation for the western provinces. Like Prime Ministers before him, Trudeau probably has no intention of promoting abolition. For one thing, he must realize that the Senate can play an important, if not federal-provincial, role in maintaining the business lobby. For another, his party reaps immense organizational benefits from appointing loyal party members to the Senate.

Provinces themselves might present obstacles to abolition. The western provinces more and more often view the Senate as a potential vehicle for greater provincial representation. They maintain this expectation despite the Senate's poor record in this role and the fact that their actual forum for grievances has been federal-provincial conferences.

Assuming that abolitionists can overcome the constitutional *impasse*, the federal government's disinterest in abolition, and the western provinces' high hopes for greater representation in the Upper House, they would still find a further obstacle in the Senate itself. Needless to say, senators would view abolition in a dim light. In addition, if abolition were included in an omnibus package which required approval of both the Senate and the House, it would threaten both the patriation of the BNA Act and an amending formula for it.

An abolition resolution, then, might have to await both patriation and an amending procedure. Presumably the amending procedure would contain a stipulation which said that amendments requiring provincial approval could be proclaimed without Senate assent.[1] This stipulation is found in Article 51 of the Victoria Charter, the draft constitution which concluded the federal-provincial negotiations of 1968-71. If the Upper House failed to pass an amendment within ninety days of its introduction, the House of Commons could override the Senate simply by passing the measure again. Under such a provision, even an intransigent Senate could not prevent abolition.

Before setting a scenario for Senate abolition, let us consider how it would affect the political system. First, the business community would lose a key forum, the Senate Banking, Trade, and Commerce Committee. While the business elite would probably continue to concentrate most of their pressure on civil servants, they would still need a second line of defence for influencing government bills. MPs, especially business reviewers, would be lobbied more often by the business community. Yet, even without tighter conflict-of-interest rules, MPs, as elected officials, will never represent business elites as exclusively as senators do now. In other words, they will never feel self-sufficient enough to overlook other publics in their constituencies to the degree that senators do. This alteration would facilitate equality of access in Canadian democracy by at last putting business interests in a competitive position similar to that of other groups.

Second, without a Senate, governments would assign more special studies to Royal Commissions. Before the rise of social investigations in the Senate, these commissions were the usual forum for such inquiries. The government might also assign more of this type of work to House-of-Commons committees. Indeed, two scholars, Robert Jackson and Michael Atkinson, have suggested that Commons committees would have greater impact if they conducted in-depth studies of policy proposals rather than clause-by-clause review of actual bills.[2] By the time a policy takes the form of a government bill and is read in the Commons, positions usually have crystallized to the point where in-depth review turns into partisan manoeuvring and posturing. The task of shifting such review to a more timely stage of the legislative process presents a challenge which the House of Commons is eventually going to have to face.

Third, political parties would miss the Senate a great deal. They would have to find other means to reward members who have distinguished themselves in public office and party work. In other systems, parties have been able to find dedicated workers even though they could not offer them rewards comparable in status, perquisites, and tenure to a Senate seat. Presumably, Canadian parties will find ways of doing the same thing.

With respect to a strategy for abolition, the dust raised in the wake of the November 15, 1976 Parti Québécois victory in Quebec will certainly have to settle before a clear picture of the future of Confederation emerges. This uncertainty, however, does not excuse us from attempting to look into the future.

Whether Quebec ultimately stays in Confederation or withdraws, one thing appears to be certain. The BNA Act, when it is patriated, will have to undergo revision. Such revision will go beyond mere incorporation of an amending procedure. It will include as well several written adjustments in the current constitutional structure. The actual contours of the amending procedure and structural changes remain, however, centres of dispute between the federal government and the provinces.

First, disagreement on procedure centres on the nature of the formula for constitutional changes which affect provinces. The Victoria Charter stated two requirements for such amendment. First, provincial legislatures rather than simply provincial governments would have to ratify them. This requirement, although it would comprise a significant enfranchisement of provincial legislatures in federal-provincial diplomacy, has not posed a stumbling block for agreement on patriation. The second requirement, however, has been a major obstacle. The Victoria Charter stipulates that support for an amendment affecting provinces must consist of the following three mandates:[3] (1) approval of each province with a population at 25 per cent of that of Canada's; (2) approval of at least two Atlantic provinces; (3) approval of at least two western provinces having together at least half the population of all western provinces. Of late, this formula has come under fire.

The British Columbia and Alberta governments both insist that their provinces be able to veto amendments; Manitoba and Saskatchewan request that any two western provinces, independent of total population, be able to veto an amendment.[4] Before the PQ victory, moreover, Quebec expressed fear that it might not retain veto power because its population might dip below 25 per cent of Canada's population.

Disputes over powers have further complicated the patriation process. Quebec scuttled the Victoria Charter in 1971 because it deemed the document too vague on protection of provincial powers in the social-legislation field.[5] Early in 1976, a "Draft Proclamation" of the federal government provided articles designed to protect linguistic and cultural rights as demanded by the Quebec government at that time.[6] The ensuing reactions of provincial Premiers indicated that they wanted a greater share of power in the areas of immigration, taxation of primary production, the powers of the federal government to declare a work within a province of general advantage to the country, creation of new provinces, communications, the Supreme Court of Canada, spending power, Senate representation, and regional disparities.[7] In addition to the changes in Senate representation mentioned above, Trudeau's response to the Premiers on January 19, 1977 opened up the possibility of: (1) a clause in a new constitution which would commit the governments to reduction of regional disparities; (2) a mandatory Federal-Provincial First Ministers' Conference each year; (3) a procedure for establishing new provinces; and (4) a method of consultation with provinces on any use of declaratory powers by the federal government. Thus, even the current federal government admits that patriation would include a restructuring of federal-provincial authority. Most pertinent for this study, however, is the fact that the federal and provincial governments alike are beginning to recognize that the patriation problem includes the future of the Senate and ongoing federal-provincial consultations.

Discussion of the ultimate shape of the constitution, once the patriation process is completed, takes us even farther into the speculative realm. None the less, three things appear fairly certain. First, the amending formula will have to meet the new concerns of the provinces. For instance, as a compromise, the constitution might have to permit two western provinces to veto amendments, and also stipulate that Quebec, independent of its population, be able to exercise a veto. Second, powers will have to be redistributed between the federal and provincial governments. Third, new mechanisms will have to be provided for federal-provincial consultation.

Abolition of the Senate fits into this scenario. Since very fundamental changes of the constitution will undoubtedly result from patriation, the argument that Senate abolition would be disruptive carries little weight today. Further, the provinces, in so far as they are interested, see the Senate as simply a *potential* vehicle for provincial representation. They might believe, in fact, that the real potential for provincial representation rests on the regularization of federal-provincial diplomacy. It is likely that, as they zero in on the need for regularization of federal-provincial consultation, they will talk much less about the number of seats that they have in the Senate and much more about shared powers and an enhanced role for federal-provincial conferences. Thus, Senate abolition dovetails with the likely scenario for constitutional reform for two reasons. First, it is only one of several radical changes being considered. Second, provinces are likely to lose interest in the Upper House's potential if they see the possibility for more regularized direct consultation between federal and provincial governments.

In a 1968 article, E. D. Briggs advocated the replacement of the Senate with a permanent "House of Provinces".[8] Patterned after the German Bundesrat, such a legislature would consist of delegates from each provincial government, and enjoy veto power over federal government bills which concern the provinces. Richard Simeon discusses the Bundesrat in his *Federal-Provincial Diplomacy*.[9] Unlike Briggs, he fails to see a Bundesrat-like House as a desirable option for Canada. Simeon describes federal-provincial diplomacy as increasingly "government of governments", whereby "legislative power is coming to rest with a group of senior federal and provincial executives, meeting as governments in formal conferences".[10] He also admits that these federal-provincial meetings could be regularized and opened to greater public scrutiny.[11] Regularization could help "government of governments" run more smoothly; more open deliberations could help build up public support for the process and assuage cynical fears that the interests of voters are abandoned when government officials and politicians meet behind closed doors. Yet Simeon ultimately dismisses a Bundesrat-like House as a forum for regularized and open "government of governments" in Canada for several reasons:[12] (1) there are comparatively few issues which become Federal-Länder disputes in Germany; (2) a great deal of the Bundesrat's work centres on purely technical matters; and (3) federal parties generally dominate Länder delegations to the Bundesrat.

Simeon's observations, which rest mainly on research conducted on the role of the Bundesrat from 1949 to 1960,[13] are neither entirely accurate nor up to date.[14] First, regarding Simeon's accuracy, the concurrent powers of the Federation and Länder encompass in fact numerous sectors of government: law and the courts; registration of births, deaths, and marriages; law of association and assembly; law relating to residence and establishment of aliens; the protection of cultural treasures; refugee matters; public welfare; citizenship in Länder; victims of wars; laws relating to economic matters; nuclear energy; labour laws and social insurance; scientific education and research; expropriation laws; nationalization of property; agricultural and forestry production; real estate; health; commodity marketing; ocean and coastal shipping; and highways and some railroads. The Bundesrat has an absolute veto in all of these concurrent sectors of governmental activity. Länder, also, frequently administer federal programs in these fields. With respect to exclusive powers of the Federation, a two-thirds vote by the Bundesrat against a bill can only be overridden by a two-thirds majority in the Lower House. Länder exercise exclusive power in education, culture, religious affairs, parts of agricultural regulation, and intragovernmental matters regarding their administrative agencies, finances, and civil servants.

Second, regarding the current validity of Simeon's observations, the decline of the centrist party in Germany, beginning in the mid-sixties, has led to a number of Bundesrat voting blocs which conflict with the majority in the Lower House. These voting blocs, which often cut across party lines, give Länder governments a major voice in federal legislation.

Briggs's proposal for a House of Provinces, therefore, merits more serious consideration in the latter part of the 1970s than when it first appeared in 1968. The current constitutional crisis points up the inevitability of a new division of powers, some of which would be concurrent, between the federal government and the provinces, and a regularization of federal-provincial consultation. Episodes such as the press corps "sit-in" during the December 1976 Federal-Provincial First Ministers' Conference dramatize the degree to which the media at least question the necessity for these meetings to be closed to public scrutiny. Recent scholarship on the German Bundesrat indicates that such an institution can be a highly effective vehicle for Länder in influencing federal policy. A House of Provinces appears to be an eminently sensible replacement for the Senate.

What would be the contours of such a Canadian House of Provinces? Briefly, provinces would receive equal representation in the House. Four seats would be allocated to each. Provinces would appoint delegates who would vote in a bloc according to the instructions of their respective governments. As in Germany, provincial Premiers and Cabinet Ministers would be the official delegates. Committees would handle much of the negotiation between provinces and federal officials. Ministers (other than House-of-Provinces members) and senior officials would often sit in for official delegates on these committees. The full House of Provinces would meet in plenary session several times a year to consider legislation which has completed the committee stage. Measures which involve concurrent powers of the federal and provincial governments would require the support of the following: (1) Quebec; (2) any province with at least 25 per cent of Canada's population; (3) two Atlantic provinces; and (4) two western provinces. With respect to matters based on exclusive powers of the Parliament of Canada, the House of Provinces could veto these only in situations where the above combination of provinces voted *against* a measure. All constitutional amendments would require the assent of the House of Commons and the *legislatures* of the same combination of provinces as above.

These proposals are meant to stimulate discussion. They follow an essential theme in this current series of books on Canadian controversies. After an in-depth analysis of Canadian senators and their legislative roles, this book urged that the Senate be abolished because it fosters a haven for the lobby from within. The state of federalism at this time suggests that we have come full circle. We saw in Chapter 1 that the creation of an Upper House in which provinces would be represented occupied a great deal of the Founding Fathers' time during the Confederation debates. The end product, the Senate, made a negligible contribution to federal-provincial relations. Traditionally, political scientists maintained that this deficiency was not dangerous to Confederation. Federal Cabinets usually included MPs from every province and voters in each province could support different parties in provincial elections from that which formed the government in Ottawa. These two ad hoc solutions served the country well for most of the first one hundred years of Confederation. Now, however, Confederation is in danger of collapse. It is time for a second attempt to regularize and to bring to public scrutiny federal-provincial relations.

NOTES

1. As cited by Donald V. Smiley in "Patriation and Amendment of the Canadian Constitution", unpublished manuscript, York University (Toronto, 1976), p. 11.
2. Robert J. Jackson and Michael M. Atkinson, *The Canadian Legislative System* (Toronto, 1974), pp. 182-83.
3. Donald V. Smiley, *Canada in Question: Federalism in the Seventies* (Toronto, 1976), p. 10.
4. Smiley, "Patriation and Amendment", p. 17.
5. Smiley, *Canada in Question*, pp. 47-48.
6. Smiley, "Patriation and Amendment", pp. 21-23.
7. A letter from Premier Peter Lougheed of Alberta to Prime Minister Pierre Elliott Trudeau as cited by Smiley, "Patriation and Amendment", p. 14.

8. E. D. Briggs, "The Senate: Reform or Reconstruction?", *Queen's Quarterly*, 75 (Spring, 1968), pp. 91-104. The idea initially came from Peyton V. Lyon in "A New Idea for Senate Reform", *Canadian Commentator* (July-August 1962).
9. Richard Simeon, *Federal-Provincial Diplomacy: The Making of Recent Policy in Canada* (Toronto, 1972), p. 302.
10. Ibid., p. 298.
11. Ibid., pp. 310-11.
12. Ibid., p. 302.
13. For example, Edward L. Pinney, *Federalism, Bureaucracy, and Party Politics in Western Germany: The Role of the Bundesrat* (Chapel Hill, N.C., 1963).
14. Guido Goldman, *The German Political System* (New York, 1974), pp. 73-76, 178-80.

Appendix I:
The Interviews

Since I based my study mostly on interviews I conducted with seventy-one out of eighty-four Canadian senators during April and May of 1971, I feel it is appropriate here to explain just how I proceeded with the interviews. As of February 1, 1977, 72 per cent of those interviewed still belong to the Senate.

OBTAINING INTERVIEWS

I originally hoped to interview all eighty-four members of the Senate, but was very happy that seventy-one senators found time to be interviewed. I received only four direct refusals. The rest of the uninterviewed senators were ill or wanted to meet me, but, for various reasons, were unable to. There is little doubt that I would not have had such success without the help of some key people. Senators Keith Davey and Jacques Flynn informed their colleagues about the research and asked for their cooperation through a circular letter. Several senators told me that they were willing to be interviewed at such length mainly because of Senator Davey's and Senator Flynn's confidence in the project. Senator Flynn's executive assistant, Ron Lefebvre, recalled his Jesuit education and stopped at nothing to make me feel at home and to facilitate my meeting senators and others on Parliament Hill. He arranged for me to have a private office, put me on Parliament's telephone-answering service, and provided a fund of inside information on how best to approach particular senators.

Mrs. Jeanne Brown, who became my bilingual assistant, was indispensable in securing interviews from French-Canadian senators. Mrs. Brown is associated with Canadian Facts and her services were arranged through Byrne Hope Sanders of the

Canadian Institute of Public Opinion and H. G. Thom of Canadian Facts. She offered a French version of the interview schedule to French-speaking senators. Since these senators feel more comfortable in French than in English, the offering of French interviews greatly increased my success rate. Even Eugene Forsey, a decidedly English-speaking senator, chose to be interviewed in French.

My task was made even easier by the atmosphere of the Senate. Mrs. Brown and myself both received a warm welcome into the "club" during our short stay. Secretaries would call us and say that now would be a good time to approach a senator. Some senators even called and asked why they had not been asked for interviews. Senator Hartland Molson, finally, "clinched" the "Most Cooperative Senator Award" when he called to tell me that he wanted to be interviewed at the very time his own hockey team, the Montreal Canadiens, was playing a crucial game in the NHL's Stanley Cup finals!

THE INTERVIEW SCHEDULE

In the interview schedule, I used a number of questions which have been used by scholars in previous studies. I also devised some questions to fit the unique requirements of research on the Canadian Senate. The sources for questions include Allan Kornberg's 1962 and 1971 surveys of the roles of Canadian MPs,[1] and a study of state legislators' roles in the U.S. by John Wahlke and colleagues.[2] The questions I employed which are not attributable to these sources were devised in 1966 with the help of F. C. Engelmann, and in 1971 with the assistance of Allan Kornberg.

Each interview started with some "ice-breakers" asking senators how they got into politics and into the Senate. Then a series of questions on their work as senators was introduced. Questions about senators' orientations toward liaison with constituents, sub-groups, and interests followed. Two fairly short sections next tapped senators' views of their roles on committees and their views of the rules-of-the-game they follow in the Upper House. In a lengthy section respondents were questioned in depth on their views of the Senate's role and of the influence they feel senators have on Parliament Hill. Two questions then followed which asked senators to summarize their political careers. The next short section was designed to find communication patterns that exist between individual senators and others on Parliament Hill. Following this, senators were asked about their relations with interest groups and parties. Next, the twenty questions which comprise the Neal scale on attitudes toward value, interest, change, and non-change in society,[3] and the "Who Am I?" question devised by Allan Kornberg and Joel Smith[4] were put. Finally, the survey concluded with a number of questions on senators' backgrounds.

Much of the interview schedule had previously been used in a 1966 study which I had conducted concerning role perceptions of Canadian senators. Since I already had this field experience with the schedule, I did not think it was necessary to retest it before embarking on the 1971 study. Some questions were omitted from the 1971 schedule, however, when it became apparent, after several interviews, that it was overly long. Copies of the final interview schedule are available upon request from me.

NOTES

1. Allan Kornberg, *Canadian Legislative Behavior* (New York, 1967).
2. John C. Wahlke *et al.*, *The Legislative System* (New York, 1962).
3. Marie Augusta Neal, *Values and Interests in Social Change* (Englewood Cliffs, N.J., 1965).
4. Allan Kornberg and Joel Smith, "Self-Concepts of American and Canadian Party Officials: Their Development and Consequences", *Polity* (Fall, 1970), pp. 70-99.

Appendix II:

STATISTICAL SUMMARY OF KEY VARIABLES—SENATORS AND MPS
(figures for MPs in brackets if different)

Variable	Range	Average Score	Test of Difference Between Senators & MPS	
			Test	Value significance
"Constituency"				
1. Population (in thousands)	14–126	77.3 (75.3)	Student's t	.72[N]
2. % of voter turnout in '68	56–90	76.6 (75.7)	"	1.01[N]
3. % of vote Liberal	16–78	48.5 (43.2)	"	2.96[B]
4. % of vote PC	6–62 (2–73)	34.0 (33.2)	"	.32[N]
5. % of vote NDP	2–57 (1–57)	13.8 (17.5)	"	2.18[C]
6. % of vote SC	1–30 (1–47)	14.1 (14.4)	"	.42[N]
7. % of vote other	1–22 (1–75)	4.7 (5.1)	"	.80[N]
8. # of ethnic groups in area	0–9	1.4 (1.5)	"	.47[N]
9. % of population urban	0–99	64.5 (57.3)	"	1.37[N]
10. Near perfect competition between parties	42.6–87.3 (6.56–90.73)	68.8 (72.8)	"	2.89[B]
11. Difference between votes won by strongest party and votes won by weakest party	1–63	22.0 (16.8)	"	2.38[C]
Province				
1. Population (in thousands)	112–7,703 (18–7,703)	3,923.8 (4,489.6)	"	1.31[N]
2. % of population urban	17–80 (0–80)	56.8 (61.1)	"	1.92[N]

			Student's t	
3. # of senators in 1971	3–23		14.9 (14.5)	.49[N]
4. *Ratio % of Senate seats held by province over % of House of Commons seats*	.4–2.8	(0–2.8)	1.3 (1.0)	" 2.94[B]
5. Near perfect competition in *% of vote* received by all parties in province	73.8–99.1		81.6 (83.2)	" 1.99[C]
6. Near perfect competition in *% of seats* in House of Commons received by all parties in province	−197.5–0		−114.5 (−118.8)	" .62[N]
7. Member's party is in a favourable competitive position in province in terms of % of votes	−54.0–33.0	(−53.0–41.0)	1.5 (2.9)	" 1.34[N]
8. Member's party is in a favourable competitive position in province in terms of *seats* in House of Commons	−100.0–100.0	(86.0–100.0)	1.6 (20.3)	" 2.79[B]
9. Province's *total proportion of representation in Parliament* in relation to population	.7–3.88		1.2 (1.1)	" 1.83[N]
10. Proportional representation in the *House of Commons* in relation to population	.9–2.93	(.9–4.56)	1.1 (1.6)	" .99[N]

STATISTICAL SUMMARY OF KEY VARIABLES—SENATORS AND MPS (Cont.)

(figures for MPs in brackets if different)

Variable	Range	Average Score	Test of Difference Between Senators & MPS Test	Value significance
11. Proportional representation in the *Senate* in relation to population	.4–6.9	1.6 (1.2)	Student's t	2.43[B]
Social Background				
1. Age	41–86 (25–77)	63.02 (49.9)	"	8.28[A]
2. Born, raised in, and represents the west	0–3	.73 (.94)	Cramer's v	.13[N]
3. Born, raised in, and represents Ontario	0–3	.75 (.95)	"	.13[N]
4. Born, raised in, and represents Quebec	0–3	.61 (.58)	"	.10[N]
5. Born, raised in, and represents Atlantic provinces	0–3	.92 (.40)	"	.25[A]
6. Raised in a city	0–1	.54 (.35)	"	.16[C]
7. Educational attainment*	0–4	1.89 (2.08)	"	.16[N]
8. Educated out of province	0–1	.27 (.42)	"	.13[C]
9. Educated out of country	0–1	.17 (.16)	"	.00[N]
10. Roman Catholic	0–1	.41 (.38)	"	.02[N]
11. Protestant	0–1	.58 (.49)	"	.07[N]

	Range	Value	(SD)	Statistic	
12. British (1=one parent; 2=two parents)	0–2	1.37	(1.00)	Cramer's v	.17[C]
13. French (1=one parent; 2=two parents)	0–2	.48	(.40)	"	.08
14. Other ethnic groups (1=one parent; 2=two parents)	0–2	.15	(.60)	"	.25[A]
15. Parents were born in Canada (1=one parent; 2=two parents)	0–2	1.56	(1.48)	"	.07[N]
16. Lawyer	0–1	.34	(.33)	"	.00[N]
17. Businessman	0–1	.27	(.26)	"	.00[N]
18. # of *firms* for which member is a director	0–23	2.62	(**)	"	**

Political Background

	Range	Value	(SD)	Statistic	
1. Liberal	0–1	.73	(.53)	"	.18[B]
2. PC	0–1	.21	(.32)	"	.09[N]
3. Has a leadership position in party's parliamentary organization	0–1	.06	(.12)	"	.08[N]
4. Has a leadership position in Parliament	0–1	.15	(.10)	"	.07[N]
5. Tenure in years	1–31	8.32	(7.23)	Student's t	1.29[N]
6. Has held *local* public office	0–1	.21	(.36)	Cramer's v	.13[C]
7. Has held *provincial* public office	0–1	.18	(.09)	"	.11[N]

STATISTICAL SUMMARY OF KEY VARIABLES—SENATORS AND MPS (Cont.)

(figures for MPS in brackets if different)

Variable	Range	Average Score	Test of Difference Between Senators & MPS	
			Test	Value significance
8. Has held *federal* public office	0–1	.31 (.01)	Cramer's v	.46[A]
9. # of levels on which member has held public office	0–3	.70 (.47)	"	.19[C]
10. Unsuccessful candidate on *local* level	0–1	.03 (.04)	"	.01[N]
11. Unsuccessful candidate on *provincial* level	0–1	.13 (.08)	"	.06[N]
12. Unsuccessful candidate on *federal* level	0–1	.20 (.10)	"	.12[N]
13. # of levels on which unsuccessful candidate	0–3	.35 (.22)	"	.15[N]
14. Has held party offices on *local* level	0–1	.21 (.49)	"	.25[A]
15. Has held party office on *provincial* level	0–1	.49 (.35)	"	.12[C]
16. Has held party offices on *federal* level	0–1	.32 (.18)	"	.14[B]
17. # of levels on which party office was held	0–3	1.03 (1.02)	"	.05[N]

Behavioural Orientations

				Cramer's v	
1. Got into politics					
a. upbringing	0–1	.54	(.41)	"	.10[N]
b. partisan motives	0–1	.34	(.59)	"	.22[A]
c. civic responsibility	0–1	.24	(.11)	"	.16[B]
2. Attempts to influence policy	0–1	.89	(.81)	"	.08[N]
3. Stays in politics					
a. psychic and personal reasons	0–1	.49	(.56)	"	.06[N]
b. civic and altruistic motives	0–1	.27	(.23)	"	.03[N]
c. desire for political influence	0–1	.51	(.33)	"	.15[B]
4. Attributes speciality to					
a. civic-altruistic motives	0–1	.24	(.15)	"	.10[N]
b. occupational expertise	0–1	.44	(.36)	"	.06[N]
c. political experience	0–1	.14	(.26)	"	.12[N]
5. Suggestions for revisions of legislation derive from					
a. civic-altruistic motives	0–1	.49	(**)	"	**
b. occupational expertise	0–1	.20	(**)	"	**
6. Main occupation is being a legislator	0–1	.61	(.72)	"	.10[N]
7. When member contacts a Cabinet Minister it is usually about					
a. a constituency matter	0–1	.14	(.71)	"	.50[A]
b. a policy matter	0–1	.45	(.43)	"	.01[N]
8. Member attributes his choice of favourite committee to					
a. civic-altruistic motives	0–1	.48	(**)	"	**
b. occupational expertise	0–1	.54	(**)	"	**

STATISTICAL SUMMARY OF KEY VARIABLES—SENATORS AND MPS (Cont.)

(figures for MPs in brackets if different)

Variable	Range	Average Score	Test of Difference Between Senators & MPs	
			Test	Value significance
Institutional Orientations				
1. Main job is constituency service	0–1	.11 (.11)	Cramer's v	.01[N]
2. Legislative focus				
a. provincial policy	0–1	.06 (.23)	"	.19[B]
b. local policy	0–1	.01 (.20)	"	.22[A]
3. Tries to find out what constituents think on issues	0–1	.82 (.90)	"	.10[N]
4. Uses structured extra-party sources for information on bills	0–1	.58 (.58)	"	.15[B]
5. Rates structured extra-party sources highly for advice	0–2	1.46 (1.03)	"	.29[A]
6. Feels accountable to extra-party institutions	0–2	1.32 (1.04)	"	.23[A]
7. Rates party sources highly for advice	0–2	.62 (.96)	"	.23[A]
8. Feels accountable to party	0–2	1.01 (.86)	"	.14[N]
9. Is expansive in the types of groups he/she consults and/or feels accountable to	0–9	4.46 (3.92)	"	.19[N]

No.	Description				Cramer's v	
10.	Member gets a large amount of mail from constituents	0–1	.49	(.78)		.27[A]
11.	Constituents communicate by phone and personal visit	0–1	.75	(.92)	"	.22[A]
12.	Communication from constituents is usually about				"	
	a. service requests	0–1	.70	(.75)	"	.04
	b. policy	0–1	.66	(.50)	"	.140[C]
13.	A cross-section of senators' province communicates	0–1	.89	(.92)	"	.03

*0=no university; 1=university, no degree; 2=university degree only; 3=graduate or professional degree; 4=graduate and professional degree.

**MP data not available.

[A]significant at 0.001 level [B]significant at 0.01 level [C]significant at 0.05 level [N]not significant at 0.05 level

Index